THE BEDFORD SERIES IN HISTORY AND CULTURE

Democracy in America

by Alexis de Tocqueville

Related Titles in
THE BEDFORD SERIES IN HISTORY AND CULTURE
Advisory Editors: Lynn Hunt, *University of California, Los Angeles*
David W. Blight, *Yale University*
Bonnie G. Smith, *Rutgers University*
Natalie Zemon Davis, *Princeton University*
Ernest R. May, *Harvard University*

The Great Awakening: A Brief History with Documents
Thomas S. Kidd, *Baylor University*

COMMON SENSE *and Related Writings by Thomas Paine*
Edited with an Introduction by Thomas P. Slaughter, *University of Notre Dame*

THE AUTOBIOGRAPHY OF BENJAMIN FRANKLIN *with Related Documents*,
Second Edition
Edited with an Introduction by Louis P. Masur, *Trinity College*

Declaring Rights: A Brief History with Documents
Jack N. Rakove, *Stanford University*

THE FEDERALIST *by Alexander Hamilton, James Madison, and John Jay:
The Essential Essays*
Edited with an Introduction by Jack N. Rakove, *Stanford University*

Creating an American Culture, 1775–1800: A Brief History with Documents
Eve Kornfeld, *San Diego State University*

*Defending Slavery: Proslavery Thought in the Old South: A Brief History
with Documents*
Paul Finkelman, *Albany Law School*

NARRATIVE OF THE LIFE OF FREDERICK DOUGLASS, AN AMERICAN SLAVE,
WRITTEN BY HIMSELF *with Related Documents*, Second Edition
Edited with an Introduction by David W. Blight, *Yale University*

ON LIBERTY *by John Stuart Mill with Related Documents*
Edited with an Introduction by Alan S. Kahan

American Social Classes in the 1950s: Selections from Vance Packard's
THE STATUS SEEKERS
Edited with an Introduction by Daniel Horowitz, *Smith College*

THE BEDFORD SERIES IN HISTORY AND CULTURE

Democracy in America

by Alexis de Tocqueville

Translated by Elizabeth Trapnell Rawlings

Abridged with an Introduction by

Michael Kammen

Cornell University

BEDFORD/ST. MARTIN'S   Boston ♦ New York

For Bedford/St. Martin's

Publisher for History: Mary V. Dougherty
Executive Editor: William J. Lombardo
Director of Development for History: Jane Knetzger
Senior Editor: Heidi L. Hood
Senior Developmental Editor: Louise Townsend
Editorial Assistant: Katherine Flynn
Senior Production Supervisor: Joe Ford
Production Assistant: Ashley Chalmers
Executive Marketing Manager: Jenna Bookin Barry
Text Design: Claire Seng-Niemoeller
Project Management: Books By Design, Inc.
Index: Books By Design, Inc.
Cover Design: Joy Lin
Cover Art: *Fourth of July Celebration in Center Square* by John Lewis Krimmel, 1819.
    The Historical Society of Pennsylvania (HSP), Prints, John Lewis Krimmel.
Composition: TexTech International
Printing and Binding: RR Donnelley & Sons Company

President: Joan E. Feinberg
Editorial Director: Denise B. Wydra
Director of Marketing: Karen R. Soeltz
Director of Editing, Design, and Production: Marcia Cohen
Assistant Director of Editing, Design, and Production: Elise S. Kaiser
Manager, Publishing Services: Emily Berleth

Library of Congress Control Number: 2008923369

For information, write: Bedford/St. Martin's, 75 Arlington Street, Boston,
    MA 02116   (617-399-4000)

ISBN-10: 0-312-46330-8
ISBN-13: 978-0-312-46330-4

Distributed outside North America by PALGRAVE MACMILLAN.

Foreword

The Bedford Series in History and Culture is designed so that readers can study the past as historians do.

The historian's first task is finding the evidence. Documents, letters, memoirs, interviews, pictures, movies, novels, or poems can provide facts and clues. Then the historian questions and compares the sources. There is more to do than in a courtroom, for hearsay evidence is welcome, and the historian is usually looking for answers beyond act and motive. Different views of an event may be as important as a single verdict. How a story is told may yield as much information as what it says.

Along the way the historian seeks help from other historians and perhaps from specialists in other disciplines. Finally, it is time to write, to decide on an interpretation and how to arrange the evidence for readers.

Each book in this series contains an important historical document or group of documents, each document a witness from the past and open to interpretation in different ways. The documents are combined with some element of historical narrative—an introduction or a biographical essay, for example—that provides students with an analysis of the primary source material and important background information about the world in which it was produced.

Each book in the series focuses on a specific topic within a specific historical period. Each provides a basis for lively thought and discussion about several aspects of the topic and the historian's role. Each is short enough (and inexpensive enough) to be a reasonable one-week assignment in a college course. Whether as classroom or personal reading, each book in the series provides firsthand experience of the challenge—and fun—of discovering, recreating, and interpreting the past.

Lynn Hunt
David W. Blight
Bonnie G. Smith
Natalie Zemon Davis
Ernest R. May

Preface

Although first published in 1835 and 1840, Alexis de Tocqueville's two-volume masterpiece, *Democracy in America*, remains the most famous and profound inquiry into the society, polity, and culture of the United States. Among hundreds if not thousands of accounts written by other foreign visitors as well as by native observers, this work endures because of the author's acute observations, keen analyses, and remarkable ability to anticipate challenges and difficulties that lay ahead for the nation and its new mode of self-governance. Tocqueville continues to amaze us with his astute predictions concerning the nation's future, ranging from racial conflict to the intense cold war rivalry between the United States and Russia, the latter considered the most astonishing of his many prophetic warnings.

Although this book must be considered and understood in its historical context—the Age of Jackson, when the young republic had begun to mature yet still suffered from growing pains of various kinds—it still speaks to our generation because of the enduring issues that Tocqueville identified and contemplated: the potential tension between liberty and equality, between the power of majorities and the rights of minorities, and between the need for civic participation and the inescapable desire for individual fulfillment. And because of his brilliance and the panoramic scope of his concerns, Tocqueville continues to be quoted and cited today with great frequency.

This edition of *Democracy in America* has been designed for instructors who want to teach this classic work but, short on time, have been reluctant to assign the full text, which normally runs to about eight hundred pages. It includes those chapters that by consensus among scholars and teachers are most famous and most representative of Tocqueville's thinking on a wide variety of issues, especially those that continue to resonate today. The selection is decidedly not present-minded, however. The aim of this abridgment has been to capture the very essence of Tocqueville's work, with roughly equal attention to both volumes, which differ in substance and tone.

To help students get the most out of their reading, the introduction offers historical and intellectual background; traces the author's journey; helps students unpack some of the meaning behind key Tocquevillian concepts such as "equality," "democracy," and "tyranny of the majority"; and offers some discussion of the work's reception, legacy, and relevance to our own time. In the appendixes, a chronology traces the key dates and events of Tocqueville's life and career; a set of questions for consideration encourages students to analyze the work from a wide variety of perspectives; and a selected bibliography directs the reader to further works by and about Tocqueville and his legacy.

Tocqueville was among the first to recognize that democracy was inevitably (he preferred the word *irresistibly*) the wave of the future for all societies, so he pondered long and hard about the opportunities, challenges, and dangers that that trend portended. *Democracy in America* is a tribute to his genius, for he knew that democracy itself was in a highly formative phase—a work in progress—and would take unanticipated forms in different societies, certainly in France and in the United States. Because of the problems he poses in *Democracy in America*, at times he almost seems to be our contemporary and his great book reads like a timely treatise concerning the challenges faced by all democracies—those already well-established and those just coming into being.

ACKNOWLEDGMENTS

I am grateful to David W. Blight, advisory editor for this series and a congenial friend of long standing, who invited me to undertake this challenging yet intriguing project. Two preeminent Tocqueville scholars, Seymour Drescher and James T. Schleifer, made suggestions concerning the chapters I proposed selecting for the abridgment, graciously indicating several that I had overlooked and others that might be safely (though reluctantly) omitted. At Bedford/St. Martin's I have been the beneficiary of expert guidance, most notably from senior development editor Louise Townsend as well as editorial assistant Katherine Flynn along with production editor Emily Berleth and Nancy Benjamin of Books By Design. As the project developed, other members of the history group at Bedford/St. Martin's—editorial assistants

Shannon Hunt and Laurel Damashek, publisher for history Mary Dougherty, and director of development for history Jane Knetzger—also provided thoughtful assistance and guidance. I am grateful to publisher Joan Feinberg and editorial director Denise Wydra for their active interest in the project.

Bedford also recruited outside reviewers to evaluate phase one of the entire project: a draft of my introduction, the edited text, and the pedagogical apparatus. All of these readers teach Tocqueville's *Democracy* in varied ways and contexts and their constructive input was invaluable. For their helpful suggestions I wish to thank David Grimsted, University of Maryland, College Park; Ellen Herman, University of Oregon; Francis MacDonnell, Southern Virginia University; Jonathan Mercantini, Canisius College; and Samuel Moyn, Columbia University.

During the fall semesters of 2006 and 2007 I taught a senior seminar at Cornell devoted to *Democracy in America* and its legacy, carrying the impact of this remarkable work right down to the present. I appreciate the students' enthusiastic participation in this effort at close reading and deeply engaged weekly discussions. I hope that History/American Studies 421 was as enlightening and as much fun for them as it was for me.

Finally, my deepest thanks go to my partner in this endeavor, Elizabeth Trapnell Rawlings, for her excellent and expeditious new translation of Tocqueville's French original. She is an expert trained in French at the University of North Carolina, Chapel Hill, and in translation at the University of Iowa. Her felicitous work and smooth collaboration served to deepen a friendship that was already well established when we decided to join ranks in tackling *Democracy.*

Michael Kammen

A Note about the Text and Translation

For this abridgment, an entirely new translation has been prepared by Elizabeth Trapnell Rawlings of Cornell University. The text being used is the thirteenth French edition, which is the last version that appeared before the author's death. It was edited for the distinguished French publisher Gallimard by J. P. Mayer (1961; reprinted in 1992).

In making selections from this very large work, I have tried wherever possible to reproduce whole chapters (or substantial segments from extremely long chapters) rather than stringing together a great many snippets drawn hither and yon. So the reader has Tocqueville's "greatest hits," as it were, but in greater depth than an extended run of famous lines and brief extracts. Because some of the chapters are quite lengthy, omissions became inevitable, and these are indicated by ellipses enclosed in parentheses. In just a few instances, the most significant portion of a chapter emerges after an extended prologue. In such cases, ellipses appear at the outset of the extract. Finally, I have omitted the cursory chapter and section synopses that appear in italics in the original work because they occupy valuable space and have limited pedagogic value. Ellipses have not been included for the omitted synopses.

A note at the beginning of each chapter indicates exactly where in the complete edition of *Democracy* the chapter will be found. All of the chapters in this edition occur in the same sequence they appear in the original work, but they have been renumbered. Nothing has been rearranged.

My goal throughout has been to respect the integrity of this great document. I have proceeded with caution and with guidance from other Tocqueville scholars.

Contents

Foreword   v

Preface   vii

A Note about the Text and Translation   xi

LIST OF ILLUSTRATIONS   xvii

PART ONE
**Introduction: Tocqueville
and His Tour de Force**   **1**

Tocqueville's Life and Character   2

The Journey in America   7

Content and Key Themes of the Work   15

How *Democracy in America* Was Received   26

The Relevance and Legacy of *Democracy in America*   29

PART TWO
Democracy in America   **35**

VOLUME I   **37**
Author's Introduction   37

Part I   **43**
1.   America's Beginnings and Their Importance for
the Future   43

2. Anglo-American Social Conditions   46

3. The Principle of the Sovereignty of the People in America   53

4. The Need to Examine What Happens in the States before
    Discussing the Federal Government   56

Part II   **62**

5. Why It Is Accurate to Say That in the United States,
    the People Govern   62

6. The Real Advantages Derived by American Society from
    Democratic Government   63

7. The Omnipotence of the Majority in the United States
    and Its Consequences   69

8. What Tempers the Tyranny of the Majority   81

9. The Principal Causes Tending to Preserve a Democratic
    Republic in the United States   84

10. A Few Remarks on Present and Probable Future
    Conditions of the Three Races Living within the
    United States   91

VOLUME II   **96**

Preface   96

**Part I: The Influence of Democracy upon the
Intellectual Development of the United States**   **98**

11. The Principal Source of Beliefs among Democratic
    Countries   98

12. The Spirit in Which Americans Cultivate the Arts   101

13. Literary Production   105

14. Certain Characteristics of Historians in Democratic
    Centuries   106

**Part II: Influence of Democracy on the Opinions
of Americans**   **109**

15. Individualism in Democratic Society   109

16. Individualism Is Greater Following a Democratic
    Revolution Than in Any Other Period   111

17. Americans Minimize Individualism with Free Institutions   112

CONTENTS

xv

18. The Role of Voluntary Associations in America   116

19. The Relationship between Associations and Newspapers   120

20. Connections between Voluntary and Political Associations   122

21. Americans Overcome Individualism through the Doctrine of Self-Interest Well Understood   126

22. The Taste for Material Comfort in America   129

23. Why Americans Appear So Restless amid Their Prosperity   131

24. How Americans' Love of Material Comfort Combines with the Love of Liberty and a Concern for Public Affairs   134

25. How Aristocracy May Result from Industry   137

Part III: Influence of Democracy on Customs as Such   **140**

26. Education of Girls in the United States   140

27. The Young Woman as Wife   142

28. How Social Equality Helps Maintain Moral Behavior in America   145

29. What Americans Mean by Equality of Men and Women   149

30. American Society Appears Both Restless and Monotonous   152

31. Why Great Revolutions Will Become Rare   154

Part IV: The Influence of Democratic Ideas and Attitudes on Politics   **161**

32. Equality Naturally Leads to a Desire for Free Institutions   161

33. The Type of Despotism Democratic Nations Have to Fear   162

34. An Overview of the Subject   167

APPENDIXES

A Tocqueville Chronology (1805–1859)   171

Questions for Consideration   173

Selected Bibliography   175

Index   177

Illustrations

1. Alexis de Tocqueville   4
2. Gustave de Beaumont   6
3. Map of Tocqueville and Beaumont's Route, 1831–1832   9
4. Beaumont's Drawing of Himself and Tocqueville with an Indian Guide   12
5. The Tocqueville Chateau in Normandy, France   26

THE BEDFORD SERIES IN HISTORY AND CULTURE

Democracy in America

by Alexis de Tocqueville

PART ONE

Introduction: Tocqueville and His Tour de Force

Alexis de Tocqueville's brilliant work, *Democracy in America*, though written nearly two centuries ago, remains the most profound and enduring study of the egalitarian society and political culture that emerged during the early republic. The work was based on Tocqueville's 1831–1832 visit to America where he and a companion traveled widely, recording their observations and experiences and conducting countless interviews, both formal and informal, with diverse Americans. Published in two substantial volumes a few years after Tocqueville's return to France, the work draws on these experiences as well as contemporary documents and historical texts to describe in meticulous detail American politics and society and the workings of the new federal system.

As we shall see, Tocqueville's impressions of America were deeply influenced by the cultural baggage he brought from his native France: an abiding fear of political instability and the repeated denial of individual liberty there as well as a strongly felt concern about despotism and the centralization of political and administrative power, all of which had shadowed his own family for several generations and pervaded the era when he came of age. Hence the immense appeal of what appeared to him, in contrast, to be the remarkable presence of political stability, individual freedom, weakness of executive power from the presidency to governorships, and the decentralization of authority in the United States. Here he clearly made miscalculations of various kinds—greatly underestimating President Andrew Jackson, for example. Indeed, because Tocqueville visited the United States in 1831–1832, we must bear in mind that *Democracy in America* is a historical text with inevitable constraints, including some inaccuracies and misconceptions, resulting from the brevity of his stay (nine months), the kinds of people who served as his most influential informants, and his inability to experience all that he had intended to. Yet, in comparing the United States with Europe in general and France in particular, Tocqueville's judgments most often were right on target.

Tocqueville's contribution in *Democracy* defies tidy categorization. Deeply interested in and informed by history, Tocqueville was also steeped in the philosophical writings of his Enlightenment predecessors, above all Montesquieu, Rousseau, and Voltaire. But whatever Tocqueville's influences, the work became a best seller almost immediately on both sides of the Atlantic, and it still speaks to our own time because of the ongoing importance of the issues Tocqueville addresses: the tensions between liberty and equality, between the power of majorities and the rights of minorities, and between the individual's need for fulfillment and the necessity of civic participation. A remarkably dispassionate and prophetic inquiry into the nature of American government and society, *Democracy in America* ranks with the works of Karl Marx, Max Weber, and Émile Durkheim, placing Tocqueville solidly in the foremost group of prominent political scientists, social theorists, and cultural anthropologists of the past two centuries, and he continues to be consulted and invoked today by writers, pundits, and politicians, often on behalf of quite different political and social agendas.

TOCQUEVILLE'S LIFE AND CHARACTER

What sort of precocious young stranger to American shores could have composed such an astonishing analysis between the ages of twenty-eight and thirty-five? His noble family dated back to the eleventh century when an ancestor fought in England alongside William the Conqueror at the Battle of Hastings in 1066. Yet the French Revolution of 1789 would have tragic consequences for this elite family. Alexis's maternal great-grandfather defended Louis XVI during his harsh trial in 1793, for which, like the king, he would die beneath the guillotine the following year. Alexis's parents also suffered imprisonment and barely escaped execution themselves, but they were released after Robespierre fell from power when the ultra-radical Terror waned. They suffered severely from incarceration, however. His father's hair turned white at the age of twenty-two, and his mother would suffer from migraine headaches, melancholy, and eventually the nervous anxiety later known as neurasthenia.

The father, Hervé, went on to study municipal law, held a series of significant administrative positions known as prefectures, recovered the family fortune after the First Republic gave way to a restored Bourbon king, and received a noble title in 1820 as a reward for dedicated public service and loyalty to Louis XVIII. When the liberal Revolution of July 1830 led to the fall of Charles X and the creation of a constitutional monarchy, however, Hervé de Tocqueville lost his privileged status and with it his commitment to civic life. He retired a disenchanted traditionalist.[1]

Alexis-Charles-Henri-Maurice-Clérel de Tocqueville was born in Paris on July 29, 1805, a third son later designated by his family to inherit the estate at Tocqueville in Normandy and entitled to be called Comte, a privilege he always declined even though he retained aristocratic sentiments. His parents were thirty-three at the time of his birth; unlike his two brothers, Alexis turned out to be a sickly and sensitive child. His early education, classical and Catholic, was provided at home near Paris by a beloved abbé who had also been his father's tutor. When Hervé became the prefect of Metz in 1820, Alexis accompanied him and entered the lycée (an advanced high school) there. At the age of sixteen Alexis began to read voraciously and broadly. Learning about the Enlightenment, especially through works by Voltaire and Rousseau, caused him to become a skeptic about the Catholic instruction he had received. For the rest of his life Alexis would wrestle with doubt about religious orthodoxy, yet remain deeply committed to the importance of religion as an essential element of social cohesion. Skepticism concerning revealed religion recurs often in his letters and personal writings.[2]

From 1824 until 1827 Alexis studied law in Paris and attended an influential series of lectures by the prominent historian François Guizot devoted to the history of civilization in Europe, which also provided a broad introduction to French history. The substance and liberal approach of Guizot's inquiry, along with the views of French antiroyalists active in the later 1820s, profoundly influenced young Tocqueville. Some of Guizot's major concerns would anticipate issues that Tocqueville addressed less than a decade later: the importance of

Figure 1. *Alexis de Tocqueville (1805–1859)*
This portrait by French lithographer Alphonse Leon Noël (1807–1884) is considered the best-known likeness of Tocqueville.

Courtesy of the Beinecke Rare Book and Manuscript Library, Yale University.

citizen participation, the positive role of civic associations, and the advantages of decentralized government.

While serving at the courts in Versailles as an unpaid junior magistrate, Tocqueville met and roomed with another young lawyer, a deputy public prosecutor named Gustave de Beaumont, with whom he formed a warm friendship.[3] Their contrasting personalities complemented one another. Where Beaumont, who came from an equally distinguished aristocratic family, was robust, genial, and outgoing, Tocqueville is described by his contemporaries as slight and reticent, "quiet and dignified, but somewhat cold." They noted his "mournful seriousness," but above all his intensity, especially where intellectual matters were concerned. He would always remain notably self-disciplined, as evidenced by his two masterworks and the speed with which he and Beaumont completed their study of prison reform following their return from the United States in 1832.[4] While Tocqueville's temperament seems to have been reserved and emotionally cautious, Beaumont appeared the effervescent one; but they bonded like the inseparable Castor and Pollux, heavenly twins in Greek mythology. Indeed, Tocqueville and Beaumont would remain lifelong friends after their sojourn in America, and Beaumont even helped oversee publication of *The Old Regime and the Revolution* while Tocqueville was in mourning for his father. When Tocqueville was gravely ill with tuberculosis, Beaumont rushed to his side and remained for five full weeks until his friend's death on April 16, 1859. Tocqueville's wife, Mary, was in very bad shape psychologically, so Beaumont's help was crucial, especially in the sensitive business of administering the last rites of the Roman Catholic Church, which had to be done in a way that would not violate any of Tocqueville's unorthodox views about religion. Following Tocqueville's premature death, Beaumont would prepare an edition of his works as an act of fraternal devotion.

When Louis-Philippe became king in 1830—a designation politically engineered by the rising bourgeois class eager to avoid social chaos from radical republicans—it meant replacing the established Bourbon line with a related one (called Orleans) that lacked legitimacy in the eyes of royalist aristocrats like the Tocquevilles and the Beaumonts. So the two ambitious young lawyers found themselves with a difficult dilemma. Although they felt obliged to swear allegiance to the new monarch in order to retain their positions, they saw little future in their legal careers and wanted to distance themselves from the seemingly precarious regime. Who knew whether it would succeed or even endure? Tocqueville and Beaumont wanted to get away—far away—so they

Figure 2.   *Gustave de Beaumont (1802–1866)*
Beaumont is shown here at the age of 35. He and Tocqueville remained
lifelong friends.
Courtesy of the Beinecke Rare Book and Manuscript Library, Yale University.

requested an extended leave of absence from the courts in order to
prepare a study of the innovative prison reforms recently taking place
in the United States. Why that particular pretext? Because French
prisons and houses of detention were notoriously disorderly, lacking
discipline and any sort of rational system. The rate of recidivism

in France was shockingly high, especially compared with what was rumored about success with repeat offenders in America. So the magistrates' request was granted, though they would have to make the trip entirely at their own expense.[5]

A passage from a letter of October 1830 clearly indicates that Tocqueville already envisioned a project larger in scope than just a report on American prisons. He aspired to fame and influence in the political sphere. He speaks of himself in the second person and speculatively about what he might achieve on this bold journey into a distant and unknown land. His mode of expression might be called the future subjunctive.

> In itself, the trip has taken you out of the most commonplace class. The knowledge you have gained in such a celebrated nation has separated you from the crowd. You know exactly what a vast republic is, why it is practicable in one place, impracticable in another [France]. All aspects of public administration have been examined one by one. When you return to France you certainly feel a strength that you didn't have when you left. If the time is favorable, some sort of publication on your part can alert the public to your existence and turn the attention of the parties to you.[6]

THE JOURNEY IN AMERICA

On April 2, 1831, our two adventurers, ages twenty-six and twenty-nine, set sail from France on an American ship named *Le Havre*. The crossing required thirty-eight days, somewhat longer than the average at that time. Three weeks into the voyage Beaumont wrote a letter to his father that clearly indicates what the young men had in mind even before they landed—though by then they had done some assiduous reading about American history and had questioned quite a few of the American passengers on board. "We have ambitious plans," Beaumont declared.

> We will see America as we survey its prisons. We will survey its inhabitants, its cities, its institutions, its mores. We will learn how the republican government works. This government is not at all well known in Europe.... Wouldn't it be good to have a book that gives an accurate notion of the American people, that paints a broad portrait of their history, boldly outlines their character, analyzes their social state, and corrects the many mistaken opinions on this subject?[7]

So initially Tocqueville and Beaumont envisioned not one but two collaborations: the first dealing with data, reports, and recommendations for prison reform in France, and the second, a far more comprehensive project that would survey American society and institutions, in part because they were so relatively new but even more to learn whether they represented what might lie ahead for France. The young men already sensed that the strength of privileged hierarchy was waning and that broader participation in public affairs must surely be the wave of the future for the Old World as well as the New. Also, given the virulent instability that had plagued France for almost half a century, what explained the apparent serenity of civic life in America? Little did they know as they crossed the choppy Atlantic (Tocqueville was seasick for the first four days and could not leave his cabin) that political conflict certainly did exist in the United States, even though it would seem notably tame to them by comparison with that in France.[8]

Nor did they anticipate that Beaumont would gradually become fascinated (and appalled) by the cruel institution of slavery in the American South, an issue that was becoming intensely politicized just on the eve of their arrival in the United States. Nat Turner's slave revolt in Virginia in 1831 frightened the slave-holding class into tightening the reins controlling the peculiar institution and then mounting an overt defense of slavery as a positive good. Abolition societies were just being organized in New England and among the Quakers of Pennsylvania, two locations where Tocqueville and Beaumont spent invaluable periods of time. Vocal figures like William Lloyd Garrison demanded immediate emancipation of all slaves.

Tocqueville shared his friend's revulsion at the mistreatment of slaves as well as of free blacks, and he also regarded the federal policy of Indian removal to locations west of the Appalachians as tragically unjust, especially coming in the wake of so many broken promises and treaty violations. Therefore he concluded Volume I in 1835 with an exceedingly long chapter, actually an addendum to the book, modestly titled "A Few Remarks on Present and Probable Future Conditions of the Three Races Living within the United States."

Beaumont was no cerebral slouch, but he regarded Tocqueville as the superior intellect. So by 1833 Beaumont would choose to leave the

Opposite: **Figure 3.**   *Map of Tocqueville and Beaumont's Journey in America (1831–1832)*

A route map adapted from George Wilson Pierson, *Tocqueville and Beaumont in America* (New York: Oxford University Press, 1938).

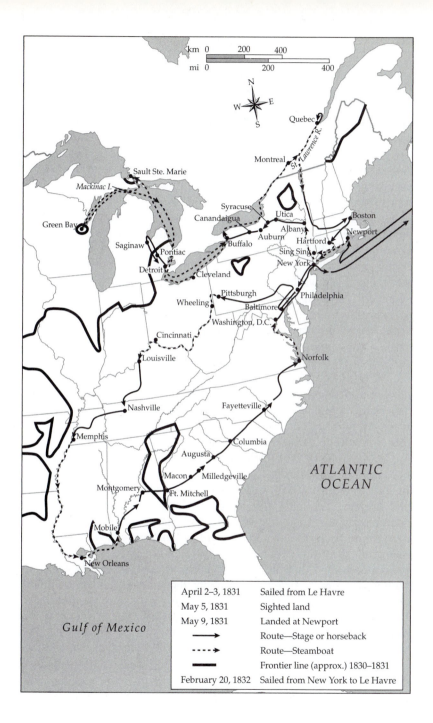

| km | 0 | 200 | 400 |
| mi | 0 | 200 | 400 |

Quebec

Montreal

St. Lawrence R.

Sault Ste. Marie

Mackinac I.

Green Bay

Syracuse

Canandaigua

Utica

Albany

Boston

Newport

Saginaw

Pontiac

Buffalo

Auburn

Hartford

Sing Sing

Detroit

Cleveland

New York

Pittsburgh

Philadelphia

Wheeling

Baltimore

Washington, D.C.

Cincinnati

Norfolk

Louisville

Nashville

Fayetteville

Memphis

Columbia

Augusta

Macon

Milledgeville

Montgomery

Ft. Mitchell

ATLANTIC
OCEAN

Mobile

New Orleans

Gulf of Mexico

April 2–3, 1831	Sailed from Le Havre
May 5, 1831	Sighted land
May 9, 1831	Landed at Newport
→→→	Route—Stage or horseback
- - -→	Route—Steamboat
▬▬▬	Frontier line (approx.) 1830–1831
February 20, 1832	Sailed from New York to Le Havre

broad-brush overview project to his friend—providing assistance
when requested—and take for his own task the writing of a lengthy
novel designed as a sharp critique of slavery and racism. The novel
appeared in 1835, some months following his friend's first volume, and
was titled *Marie, ou l'esclavage aux États-Unis: Tableau de moeurs
américaines* (*Marie, or Slavery in the United States: A Depiction of
American Customs*). Like *Democracy in America*, the novel was well
received despite appearing in two volumes and containing lengthy
notes as well as appendixes.[9]

Strong ministerial pressure in September to return to France early
would reduce the fifteen to eighteen months that Tocqueville and
Beaumont had hoped to spend in America to nine. That would barely
be adequate for them to complete the ambitious project they envisioned
when they planned their trip; and even the nine months that they did
spend in North America is deceptive because they suffered several
serious travel delays once they left the settled cities of the eastern
seaboard for the trans-Appalachian West and the South. The winter of
1831–1832 turned out to be one of the coldest on record. The Ohio
and Mississippi rivers froze to an unprecedented extent, impeding
their travel from Louisville to New Orleans and causing all sorts of illness and vexing stops that meant their intended time in the South,
especially, would be radically reduced. Even so, the distance they
managed to cover and the feel for the country they gained as a whole
turned out to be remarkably extensive.

On May 9, 1831, they landed prematurely at Newport, Rhode Island,
because food and supplies had run so low on the ship. Two days later
they arrived in New York City, where they remained for several weeks
and gained their initial glimpse of a society they would describe as
commercially oriented, materialistic, and energetic. American restlessness would become a persistent motif in *Democracy in America*. Their
many letters of introduction promptly opened doors, and because the
press proclaimed their arrival with considerable fanfare, they literally
"suffered" from a surfeit of attention: dinners, dances, and celebra-
tions of various sorts. That would become a pattern throughout their
tour and facilitate the collection of information, much of it received
orally along with an inundation of public documents, prison-related as
well as ones more general in nature that they requested.

While settled in New York Tocqueville and Beaumont began their
systematic tour of prisons, first in the City and then at Sing-Sing over-
looking the Hudson River (May 29 through June 7), an institution actually built with convict labor and based on a new system of absolute

prisoner silence and very strict discipline enforced by physical punishment, most notably using the whip (or "cat" as it was called). By early July they had reached Albany and, as guests of honor at an elaborate celebration of the Fourth, were deeply affected by the heartfelt expressions of patriotism they witnessed. After listening to the customary reading of the Declaration of Independence for the entire assemblage, Tocqueville summed up his awed response with this description.

> It was as though an electric current moved through the hearts of everyone there. It was in no way a theatrical performance. In this reading of the promises of independence that have been kept so well, in this turning of an entire nation toward the memories of its birth, in this union of the present generation with one that is no longer and with which, for a moment, it shared all these generous feelings, there was something profoundly felt and truly great.[10]

And yet, at several points in *Democracy* Tocqueville would comment negatively about American chauvinism. A few weeks prior to that impressive celebration in Albany, Tocqueville had written to his mother, "These people seem to me stinking with national conceit; it pierces through all their courtesy"; and variations on that theme would appear throughout his correspondence.[11] Nevertheless, the love of country manifest in Albany and elsewhere genuinely moved the young visitor from a country where partisan divisions remained so strong over the relative merits of monarchy versus republicanism. Americans seemed united in their gratitude for independence as well as the novel form of government to which it gave rise.

From Albany the travelers headed west by coach on very rough roads, utterly amazed by their first full glimpse of largely unfelled American forests. Their route took them through the Mohawk Valley to Utica, next to Syracuse on July 7, and then to Auburn, where they toured another newly "reformed" prison. In nearby Canandaigua they met with John Canfield Spencer, a member of the New York legislature who answered countless questions about state government, politics, the judicial system, and numerous other matters of interest to the two magistrates. Spencer would be one of Tocqueville's most influential sources and wrote the introduction to the first American edition of *Democracy* (1838).[12]

Tocqueville and Beaumont moved on to brief stops in Buffalo, Cleveland, and Detroit, where they learned of an opportunity to make their way on horseback, truly roughing it, all the way to Pontiac and

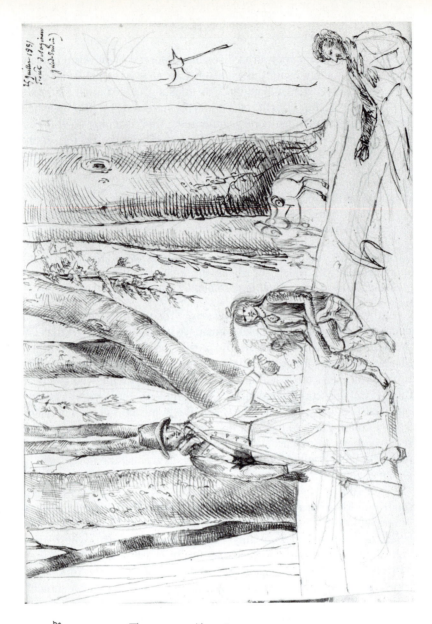

Figure 4.
Gustave de Beaumont's drawing of "The Guide and the Osier Bottle," July 29, 1831

A few months into the sojourn, Beaumont captured this moment along the trail when he and Tocqueville and their guides stopped for a break in the forest near Saginaw, Michigan. Tocqueville is at the right leaning against the fallen tree. Beaumont hands some liquid refreshment to the guide.

Courtesy of the Beinecke Rare Book and Manuscript Library, Yale University.

ultimately Saginaw, Michigan, then a remote and primitive outpost. They did so, and for their hardship they achieved two goals: experiencing the forest primeval and Native Americans in something resembling their original habitat. Tocqueville chronicled their adventures in an extended account titled "Two Weeks in the Wilderness."[13]

Following their return to Detroit Tocqueville and Beaumont made a steamboat excursion to Mackinac Island in Michigan and then to Green Bay, Wisconsin. After retracing their route once more to Detroit they continued to Niagara Falls, which was already a popular tourist destination.[14] From there the pair headed north by northeast "down" the St. Lawrence River to Montreal and Quebec City, where they felt very much at home and where the social homogeneity of a traditional Catholic community delighted them. Those were notably happy weeks, not only because they were surrounded by French speakers but also because the sense of tradition and serenity appealed to their nostalgia for a way of life that seemed to be rapidly waning in France and compared most favorably with the intensely commercial breakneck pace of life in the United States. The "habitants" of Lower Canada, as Quebec was called, seemed contented rather than restlessly on the go like the Americans.[15]

From there it did not take long to make their way south via Lake Champlain to western Massachusetts and then to Boston. That venue became a highlight of the entire journey because of conversations they held with leading authorities on American history and law centered there: prominent figures such as Jared Sparks of Harvard College, Senator Daniel Webster, and former president John Quincy Adams (now serving in Congress and an outspoken opponent of slavery), as well as such leading members of the clergy as William Ellery Channing, the distinguished Unitarian spokesman. Each one was subjected to a barrage of questions from the two visitors, but especially on issues most germane to his area of particular expertise, such as Sparks on the origins of local government in New England and Channing on religious diversity and toleration in the United States.

In October 1831, Philadelphia by way of New York (once again) would be their next major destination. Everything about Philadelphia fascinated them, from the tidy grid of the streets, with numerals rather than names for identification, to the strong emphasis on philanthropy. Having seen several more prisons in the Boston area, Tocqueville and Beaumont now grew weary of all the places of incarceration and alms they felt compelled to visit in the Quaker City. Nevertheless, in his relentless quest for authentic and reliable information, Tocqueville proceeded to interview countless prisoners one on one to learn their life histories, the nature of their crimes, and their opinions of the new and innovative Eastern State Penitentiary. (Many had previously been imprisoned elsewhere.)[16]

From Philadelphia they made their way to Baltimore on October 28, where they experienced the urban South and witnessed slave society for the first time. This would be the pivotal point for Beaumont, who became so enraged and distressed by the inhumanity of American racism that he determined to shape his own book project accordingly. Returning to Philadelphia briefly, Tocqueville and Beaumont next made their way westward across Pennsylvania to Pittsburgh, from there to Wheeling in what was still part of Virginia, and then down the Ohio River, arriving on December 1 in Cincinnati, already considered the "gateway to the West." More bustling commerce greeted them there.

During the cruel winter of 1831–1832 they struggled to reach and see the South, but because the elements and rough, often impassable roads conspired against them they were only able to reach Nashville, eventually Memphis on the Mississippi, and, finally, when the great river thawed, boarded a grand steamboat to New Orleans (arriving on January 1, 1832), where their visit had to be foreshortened. Despite the brevity of their visit, they were shocked to learn how common it was for white men to enjoy the company of beautiful mixed-race mistresses, a pattern of behavior that seemed to be public knowledge and casually accepted.

Thereafter, because their time was growing so frustratingly short, they stopped only briefly in Mobile, the Gulf port, and then moved swiftly by stagecoach east and north across Alabama, Georgia, and the Carolinas; from Norfolk they caught a vessel to Washington, D.C., their last major stop, arriving on January 17. Once again they received warm hospitality, as they had throughout the trip, and met with many prominent individuals, ranging from President Andrew Jackson for an interview, who impressed them not at all, to Secretary of State Edward Livingston, who did. They made excellent use of their free passes to visit Congress and spent many hours at the Capitol, listening to and conversing with public figures.[17]

After little more than two weeks in the federal city they moved swiftly to New York to gather the trunks of printed matter and clothing they had stored there, enjoyed a gala round of farewell parties, and sailed for France on February 20. They wrote so little on the trip home and immediately upon arrival that we do not even know the actual date of their return to Le Havre. But Tocqueville was back in Paris by April 4, having spent 271 days in the United States and 15 in Canada.

CONTENT AND KEY THEMES OF THE WORK

Readers of *Democracy in America* should keep in mind that the book was written, first and foremost, for a French rather than an American audience, though over the intervening generations a predictable reversal has occurred. French students are more likely to read Tocqueville's later work published in 1856, *The Old Regime and the Revolution*, which explains a pivotal time in their own history, while American students are far more likely to explore and assess *Democracy in America*.

One of Tocqueville's greatest and most significant strengths is his comparative vision. When he wrote about the United States, he did so with implications for his own country constantly in mind. In September 1831 he observed in a travel notebook that "in America, free *moeurs* [mores] have created free institutions; in France, free institutions must create free *moeurs*."[18] That would become a central theme of the entire work. In Volume II (1840), which is less descriptive and more theoretical than Volume I (1835), Tocqueville often notes the consequences of a democratic society for the political process, and while chapter titles may refer to the United States, he routinely has France in mind, often drawing on observations he has made of social or political change at home.[19]

When Tocqueville was still in his early twenties, having just completed his legal studies, he traveled to Switzerland, Rome, Naples, and Sicily, taking more than 350 pages of notes along the way. As Beaumont would observe after Tocqueville's death, his inquiries and speculations "always had a practical and definite object. . . . He considered the past only as it affected the present, and foreign countries only with a view to his own." Tocqueville himself insisted on this basic goal and method in an 1843 letter to one of his closest friends, Louis de Kergorlay: "It was always by noticing likeness or contrasts that I succeeded in giving an interesting and accurate description of the new world. . . . I believe the perpetual silent reference to France was a principal cause of the book's success."[20]

Despite his assumption that popular sovereignty—consent of the governed—represented the wave of the future, Tocqueville believed that the specific forms of democratic institutions would have to be adapted to respective national histories and idiosyncrasies. In France, for example, Tocqueville believed that liberty and the established church had long been at odds, whereas in America, he found, religious diversity and commitment tended to provide a major bulwark for democracy. The spirit of religion and the spirit of liberty reinforced one another admirably.

The relationship among religion, democracy, and liberty is especially critical to our understanding of what Tocqueville noticed, valued, and ultimately concluded about America. His highest priority, always, was the achievement of liberty because he feared despotism of any kind, whether it arose from the tyranny of an individual, such as a king or an emperor, or from the mob. His name will forever be associated in democratic theory with the phrase "tyranny of the majority," a notion that was actually suggested to him by one of his most important American sources, Jared Sparks, the distinguished historian at Harvard College and later its president.[21]

Tocqueville and his family had known and suffered from political instability for three generations, so he understandably regarded it as the great nemesis of individual liberty. Instability had deprived family members and friends of their lives, their positions in society as well as in civil life, and, consequently, their liberty. Religion in the New World, however, both in the diversely Protestant United States and in Roman Catholic Quebec, seemed to be a major source of social cohesion and therefore of stability. Religious commitment did much to provide for a high level of morality, which in turn sustained stability in a way that seemed far more real and tangible to Tocqueville than the abstract notion of virtue which had been central to Enlightenment thinking, especially among those who led and legitimized the American Revolution.

If religion underpinned civil equality and social stability, and the latter was a prime requisite for liberty, then Tocqueville, despite his everlasting personal doubts, would heartily applaud the positive role of religion in American life. Because power, especially in the wrong hands, threatened liberty, Tocqueville would make observations like the following in *Democracy*: "Omnipotence in itself seems to me a bad and dangerous thing. Exercising it seems to me beyond the power of any man, whoever he is, and I think only God can safely be called all-powerful, because his justice and wisdom are always equal to his power."[22] From his Introduction to Volume I the reader would never imagine that Tocqueville might be a skeptic. We must assume sincerity when he writes that "God need not speak to us directly for us to grasp the clear signs of his will; we need only examine the usual course of nature and the continuous flow of events; I know, without a word from the Creator, that the stars in outer space are following the arc traced by His fingers."[23]

Tocqueville perceived three major forms of influence giving shape to democracy in America. The first was geography, which blessed the country with vast resources and hence economic opportunities that would enhance equality but also provide isolation from enemies and the conflicts as well as the deeply ingrained traditions of the Old World. The second element was law along with a judiciary and jury system that grew in his esteem as he came to be informed by people such as Joseph Story, associate justice of the Supreme Court, and the multivolume *Commentaries on American Law* by Chancellor James Kent of New York. The third, and most important, he called *moeurs*, a word that Tocqueville himself used in different ways in diverse contexts. Therefore, some definitions are in order.

The simplest translation of *moeurs* is mores, but that does not take us very far, particularly because mores can refer to customs, manners, and the routine beliefs of a people, ranging from secular values to the practice of religion. Tocqueville tells us that by *moeurs* he means "habits of the heart" as well as the ideas and opinions that "constitute their character of mind." Two key words that recur throughout his text then, *customs* and *mores* (what anthropologists frequently refer to as culture), are meant to indicate "the entire moral and intellectual state of a nation."[24] The young author made it very clear that physical advantages, enacted legislation, and even the Constitution itself did not matter as much as mores in sustaining democratic habits and institutions. As he wrote in the margins of a notebook that he carried on his travels, "Mores are the only tough and durable power among a people."[25]

Closely related and equally important, if not more so, is Tocqueville's use of the word-concept *democracy*—elusive and problematic for us because the inferences it carries in his work shift, and taken together may seem ambiguous. What needs to be understood, above all perhaps, is that its meaning was less political than social. Basically, in his usage it usually refers to equality and the voice of the people rather than to a particular system of political or governmental institutions. Social equality had led to the potential equality of participation in civic life. As George Wilson Pierson, a preeminent Tocqueville scholar put it, the author meant "equality in social and economic conditions as well as in political: equal privileges in government, equal civil rights before the law, equal economic benefits, equal intellectual training, no classes of any kind, even the disappearance of distinctions in fashion and 'society'." Tocqueville's "democracy" embraced all of that. He knew perfectly well that women and most African Americans and Native Americans could not vote. But compared with the stringent and exclusionary property requirements for voting in Europe, the United States seemed to this visitor to be governed by popular sovereignty. Because property was so much more accessible in the United States than in France, the American electorate was constantly expanding.[26]

In June 1831, when Tocqueville had been in America for only a few weeks, he sent a lengthy letter to his confidant Louis de Kergorlay, describing his initial impressions and reflections. *Démocratie*, he wrote, "is either broadly advancing in certain states or as fully extended as imaginable in others. It is in the *moeurs*, in the laws, in the opinion of the majority."[27] In the years that followed he would elaborate on that point of departure, and he would open his Introduction to Volume I in 1835 with the now familiar assertion: "Of all the novel features that drew my attention during my stay in the United States, the most striking was the equality of conditions." As the reader will see, he then elaborated the broad-gauge influence of this "fundamental fact." Many other aspects of American democracy flowed from it.[28]

Later, as Tocqueville began work on Volume II of *Democracy*, he wrote yet another, even more revealing letter to Kergorlay. "To indicate to men," he declared, "if it is possible, what they must do in order to escape from tyranny and degeneration while becoming *equalitarian*, such is, I think, the general idea which epitomizes my book [Volume I] and which will appear on every page of the one that I am writing [Volume II]. To labour in this direction is in my eyes a holy occupation, and one in which one must spare neither one's money, nor one's time, nor one's life."[29]

It is crucial to appreciate that initially Tocqueville lacked very much enthusiasm for political democracy, manifest as universal suffrage. It evoked doubts every bit as much as religious belief did. His instinctive stance was that of a skeptic. Yet he did believe from the outset that a democratic revolution was "irresistible," by which he meant inevitable, and that because it was already much more advanced in the United States than in France, he might be able to envision the future prospects for democracy as a viable way of life by assessing its strengths and weaknesses in the place where they would be most apparent. As John Stuart Mill, the prominent English philosopher and libertarian, observed in his rave review of Volume I, Tocqueville's purpose was "not to determine whether democracy shall come, but how to make the best of it when it does come." Tocqueville made his basic assumptions quite apparent in a letter:

I am as profoundly convinced as one can be of anything in this world that we are irresistibly drawn by our laws and our mores toward an almost complete equality of social conditions. Once social conditions are equal, I no longer see any intermediary stage between a democratic government (and by the word democratic I mean not a republic but a state of society in which everyone, to a greater or lesser degree, takes part in the political process) and the unchecked rule of one man. I don't doubt for a moment that in time we will arrive at one or the other.[30]

Tocqueville would make that explicitly clear in his Preface to Volume II in 1840, but this time to advise his readers just exactly where he stood personally concerning his chosen subject. "Given the fact that I strongly believe the democratic revolution we are witnessing today is irresistible," he explained, "and that it would be neither desirable nor wise to resist, it may be surprising that, in this book, I have frequently written harsh words about the democratic societies created by this revolution. I would reply that it is because I was not in any way an enemy of democracy that I have tried to be honest about it."[31]

By 1834–1835, in fact, Tocqueville had actually become more sympathetic toward democracy, however hesitantly, in ways and to a degree that neither he nor we could have anticipated when he left France in 1831. Here is how he concluded the principal text of Volume I: "Should we not then think about the gradual development of democratic institutions and values, not as something better but as the only means left to us of remaining free; and without loving democratic government, would we not be inclined to adopt it as the best and most honest solution to the social evils of today?"[32]

More than a decade after Tocqueville's death, Henry Reeve, the very young Englishman who made the first translation of *Democracy* directly following the appearance of each volume, had this to say in an extended essay about the author who had become a close personal friend.

Because M. de Tocqueville based his literary and political reputation on the study of democracy and democratic institutions, it was hastily inferred that these institutions were the object of his own predilections. Because he described with perfect impartiality the means by which the American people appeared to have succeeded in combining a highly democratic state of society with a free and regular government, it was supposed that M. de Tocqueville carried a love of democracy to the length of republicanism. Even among some of his intimate friends an opinion existed that his political principles had in them something extreme and revolutionary, and his own family, ardently attached to the royalist party in France, were half alarmed at the audacity and the fame of the most illustrious member of their house.[33]

Tocqueville's affirmation of democracy then, however hesitant or critical it might be at times, was firmly rooted in his fear of tyranny and especially the "unlimited authority of a single man," a reality that had been experienced under Robespierre and Napoleon, and would be once again under Napoleon III less than two decades later. As we have noted, Tocqueville's greatest goal and strongest commitment was to liberty, "by taste," yet he never fully defined what he meant by it, much less developed a theory of it. We can say with assurance, however, that liberty meant the capacity to pursue one's own ideas and abilities freely even when they diverged from those that were dominant at any given time. Moreover, social and political disorder invariably meant the absence of freedom. As a leading Tocqueville authority recently observed, liberty was an inexplicable attachment that Tocqueville could scarcely describe for those who did not share his ultimate passion. John Stuart Mill shared that passion, which helps to explain his long and totally sympathetic reviews of both volumes.[34]

Like most of his contemporaries, Tocqueville believed in the existence of national character. He never doubted that the French possessed such an identifiable profile, as did the English, the Scots, the Germans, the Italians, the Swiss, and others (even though Germany and Italy did not yet even exist as unified nation-states in 1832).[35] One significant aspect of his mission to the United States was to determine the American character, and he makes frequent reference in his text and correspondence to qualities that he regarded as distinctively American. That is not a fashionable perspective in our own time, at least not according to most scholars;[36] yet it certainly does persist among the general public, and we need to understand that in Tocqueville's mind it was second nature to perceive such attributes and ascribe them to a combination of environment, custom, and race (yet another word whose usage seems odd to us).

When he used the word *race*, he did not mean what we normally do, but would casually refer to the French race, or to the English. He was less likely to do so in the American context because he recognized that numerous backgrounds had contributed to the population of the United States. Even so, one stock seemed to predominate in his view, not just numerically but in terms of influence by means of law, language, and custom. Therefore he often used "Anglo" in some combination (most often Anglo-Americans) to indicate the group that provided those living in the United States with their distinctive characteristics.[37] In analyzing and discussing Tocqueville's work, we need to avoid projecting our perspectives and assumptions on to his generation. He was, after all, a comparative sociologist fascinated by differences as well as similarities. He hoped to understand, for example, which customs and institutions that worked so successfully in their American context might prove equally viable at home in his own — despite historical differences in context and "character."

Many of Tocqueville's most important and well-known observations arose from his sense of profound differences between the two countries and their cultures. Government in France, for example, was exceedingly centralized, perhaps overly so. In the United States, by contrast, government seemed to Tocqueville so decentralized as to be barely visible and minimally intrusive in domestic life. (He differentiated between *administration*, which involved assessing and collecting taxes, and *government*, which referred to such actions as maintaining order through police power.) The existence of political associations, but above all the ubiquitous presence of American *civic* associations, seemed utterly extraordinary and unprecedented — so much so that Americans appeared to Tocqueville like a nation of "joiners." To someone who feared an excess of "individualism" (the very word actually originated in English with Tocqueville) and hence the privatization of civic life, the proliferation of associations looked like a splendidly positive development. Tocqueville explored the paradox that democratic individuals lack adequate time for politics because of their commercial ambitions, yet they nonetheless need and want political stability as a framework for their private pursuits.[38]

What Tocqueville perceived as the homogeneity of public opinion as well as its sheer force in America worried him, and the rapidly growing role of the press in disseminating public opinion seemed equally a matter for praise as well as concern because his passion for liberty meant that acceptance of diverse views was essential. Would Americans be able to tolerate political and ideological differences as readily as they seemed to accept religious diversity? It troubled Tocqueville profoundly that Americans cherished equality even more than liberty. As he phrased it, "When citizens are almost all equal, it becomes difficult for them to defend their independence from the aggressions of authority."[39]

Lesser issues prompted critical responses as well. Because Americans were so practical and empirical, they had an aversion to what

Tocqueville called "general ideas," the quest for which was his own great strength, of course, but also a quality that he regarded as quintessentially French. Americans honored practice over theory. The latter lacked engaging appeal. Because they were so busily in quest of wealth (Tocqueville mentions "love of money" frequently), they had too little time for public affairs. American women, especially married women, seemed virtuous, almost to the point of excessive modesty. (Tocqueville had his first love affair as a teenager and was not always faithful to his English-born wife, Mary Mottley, who was nine years his senior.) Americans did not routinely drink wine with dinner, which seemed positively uncivilized! And so it went. The customs of the country that he visited seemed so often to be in marked contrast with those of his own.

There was also much that Tocqueville admired in the United States, as we shall see. He felt that, overall, Americans were the best educated people in the world. Few were highly educated, but even fewer were illiterate or altogether ignorant. Above all, American political institutions seemed to work remarkably well, especially the pattern of checks and balances, the jury system, and local government. By and large, Americans had orderly habits, violence was rare (he wrongly believed), cruelty was not common (compared with France), and property seemed more secure than in France. As he concluded at the end of Volume II, typically seeking balance: "I see that the benefits and the evils are about equal in the world."[40]

Still other concepts and emphases recur prominently throughout this work. Beyond "equality of condition" and the existence of "a middling standard," when Tocqueville refers to the "democratic revolution" he often means more than the American, the French, and the subsequent rebellion and independence of Spain's colonies in the New World—which were manifest political events. He also had in mind the long-term socioeconomic changes that began to arise in the seventeenth and eighteenth centuries as the development of capitalism produced a prosperous merchant class and then, gradually, a middle class that would be most evident in the United States. He believed that prosperity sustained stability, which in turn helped to support a democratic society.[41]

Chapter 7 in Volume I, dealing with the power of the majority and its consequences, is notably important and has been highly influential and endlessly discussed. As Tocqueville asserts at the outset, "The absolute sovereignty of the majority is the essence of democratic government; in a democracy, nothing outside the majority is capable of mounting resistance to it." He then adds that most of the state constitutions have sought to artificially increase this natural strength of the majority. He also calls attention to the *moral* authority of the majority, noting that it rests at least partially "on the principle that the interests of the greatest number must be preferred to those of the few." That brings him to his justly famous concern about the potential for tyranny by the majority, a menace that could best be countered by a proper regard for justice, especially concerning individual rights. He called it "the sovereignty of the human race" over that of the people.[42] In brief, universal ideals of fairness took priority over norms of the political process.

Later in the same famous chapter Tocqueville describes a particularly insidious form of mind control: the power exercised by the majority in America over *thought*, and he insists that nowhere else in the world is there "less independence of mind and real freedom of debate than America." Historians and others have disputed this contention, pointing to the remarkable proliferation of newspapers and journals during the antebellum period, which often meant that each political party and many religious denominations had their own organs of opinion.[43] Tocqueville himself even devoted a chapter of Volume I to Freedom of the Press in the United States!

He also confided to an inquiring friend in France that consensus on the fundamentals of government seemed a very positive situation, especially compared with the sheer amount of conflict at home concerning the optimal form of government.

> What strikes me is that the immense majority of people are united in regard to certain common opinions. So far, that is what I have envied most about America. To begin with, I have not yet been able to overhear in a conversation with anyone, no matter to what rank in society they belong, the idea that a republic is not the best possible government, and that a people does not have a right to give itself whatever government it pleases. The great majority understands republican principles in the most democratic sense.[44]

Inevitably and understandably, Tocqueville did not get everything quite right, whether we look at his interpretations of what he encountered, the sources he relied on, or theoretical conclusions that he reached. Although brilliant and learned, he was also quite young and his time in North America was brief. His working notes include some wonderfully disarming concessions, such as: "I assert this idea without proving it."[45] Starting with sources, he relied rather heavily on more conservative members of the American elite, such as Sparks and

Kent. Their fear that an excess of democracy would lead to mediocrity was picked up by Tocqueville because it was congenial to him, and such concerns often pervade his text. His tradition-oriented sources felt a romanticized nostalgia for the Revolutionary generation, regarded their own as less capable than its predecessors, and worried about the prospect of mob rule. That is why they so disliked Andrew Jackson's egalitarianism. Tocqueville's insistent emphasis on "equality of condition" was misleading, though he actually modified it late in Volume I. He knew perfectly well that there were rich and poor, but he believed that, unlike in Europe, these were not permanent conditions.

By comparing the notebooks that Tocqueville kept while traveling with the ultimate text of *Democracy*, we know that he sometimes copied out almost verbatim what an authoritative or impressive informant had told him. He did not always have time to seek alternative views, though in fairness it must be noted that he addressed certain fundamental questions, such as the role of religion, to as many contacts as possible.[46] Still, his quest for authoritative sources caused him to favor certain texts and perspectives over others.

He also placed far too much emphasis on the curtailment of primogeniture and entail in America as a primary cause of "equality of condition."[47] He had been led to believe that inheritance laws were changed dramatically as a *result* of the Revolution, so that a father would be compelled to divide his land equally among his heirs. Primogeniture, by which a family estate passed in its entirety to the eldest son, had in fact been largely abandoned well *before* the American Revolution, as had the tight restrictions on alienating land from a family (entail). Moreover, only when the head of a household died without a will (intestate) did laws provide a formula for equitable support of his widow and children. The nature of restrictions affecting the transmission of property involved complexities (and New World simplifications as well) that Tocqueville simply did not fully comprehend.[48]

His strongly held belief that the central (federal) government was so weak as to be virtually invisible flies in the face of Andrew Jackson's imperious destruction of the Second Bank of the United States, his ability to prevail over South Carolina's desire for Nullification of the high protective tariff, and his tragic determination, along with that of Congress, to relocate major Native American tribes from the southeastern United States to lands beyond the immediately desired area of white settlement (a policy well-known to Tocqueville).[49]

Tocqueville simply accepted without hesitation Jared Sparks's view that the seedbed of American democracy could be found among the earliest colonists to arrive in the seventeenth century. Men of wealth and high social status actually exercised a considerable degree of authority and power, as did the clergy, which has prompted scholars to describe colonial life as a silent democracy in the face of a speaking aristocracy. Tocqueville also subscribed to what subsequently became the Horatio Alger myth that many wealthy people in the United States were self-made, starting from humble beginnings. We know that in reality a great many of the affluent families in antebellum times had inherited more than a nest egg. They did not start from scratch.[50]

The second volume of *Democracy* was not as widely read as the first. It is more abstract, more speculative, and "darker" in terms of the author's sense of what democracy might offer by way of improvement in civil society. It is guardedly enthusiastic about democratic polities and warns of potential "dangers" in the implementation of republican government.[51] It places greater emphasis on the implications of equality and how those developments are likely to affect society, politics, and culture. Because its texture and tone differ from the first volume, some scholars have argued that they really are two distinct, almost disconnected pieces of work. Others, however, acknowledge these differences but remain more impressed by the continuities and consider the two volumes as a singular, cohesive, and coherent project.[52]

Volume II does, however, contain a famous passage devoted to what the author called "the doctrine of self-interest properly understood," a theory with seemingly upbeat implications in explaining why democracy just might prove to be viable in the United States. Basically, Tocqueville rejected the eighteenth-century belief that a successful republic required a virtuous citizenry. Taking a more realistic view of human nature, he observed that Americans are quite willing to show "how enlightened selfishness leads them to help each other and inclines them to sacrifice both time and money for the good of the State."[53] (When Tocqueville became deeply involved in planning a republican constitution for France in 1848, he kept the American Constitution of 1787 very much in mind. Although he advocated bicameralism, he lost that battle because such a dual arrangement was simply too foreign to French tradition.[54])

The principle of self-interest properly understood would establish a balance between public and private interests by showing how concern for the interests of others could, in the long run, also serve one's own interest.[55] Tocqueville felt some ambivalence about the validity of that notion, yet gave it enough credibility to persuade his audience and generate considerable discussion ever since. Because the concept of

Figure 5.   *The Tocqueville Chateau in Normandy, France*
This photograph shows the Tocqueville family's ancestral estate in Normandy.
It was here that Tocqueville wrote Volume II of *Democracy in America.*
Courtesy of the Beinecke Rare Book and Manuscript Library, Yale University.

self-interest properly understood is so pivotal to the author's sense of
why democracy seems to work in the United States, that chapter
requires especially careful consideration.[56]

HOW *DEMOCRACY IN AMERICA* WAS RECEIVED

The reception of his work exceeded Tocqueville's expectations though
not his aspirations. First, the Prison Report won its coauthors the Mont-
yon Prize in 1833 and was reissued in 1836 and 1844—not bad for a
public policy document. Volume I of *Democracy* appeared in January
1835 and went through countless printings, astonishing even the publisher, who had never even bothered to read the manuscript. It was
translated almost immediately into English and Spanish. Volume II,
which is more theoretical and less descriptive as well as less hopeful
about the implications of democracy, was not so warmly reviewed; yet

with completion of the entire work translations also appeared in German, Danish, Russian, and Serbian. It became an instant classic of political theory, and it received a prize of 8,000 francs from the Académie Française, the nation's most elite group of intellectuals (limited to forty members), which elected Tocqueville to membership in 1841. In 1838, on the strength of Volume I alone, he had been elected to the Academy of Moral and Political Science. By mid-century he had become what the French call "an immortal" and internationally famous.

As the reader will soon see, Tocqueville said many uncomplimentary things about Americans and their country. Most germane here, perhaps, he repeatedly observed that they disliked criticism and therefore called them thin-skinned.[57] How then can we explain the overwhelmingly positive reception the work received in the United States? The answer is reasonably clear. There had been numerous books by foreign visitors published during the dozen years preceding 1840 and, almost without exception, they contained harsh critiques on subjects ranging from American manners and hospitality to the sheer discomforts of existence in such a "primitive" environment. The best known among these disapproving tourists were Captain Basil Hall (1829), Frances Trollope (1832), Harriet Martineau (1837), and Frederick Marryat (1839). Tocqueville resolutely refused to read any traveler's account while working on his own because he did not want to risk being influenced in any way by the observations and opinions of others.

Tocqueville at least balanced his criticisms and concerns with commendations, some of them even high praise. To cite just one example from the first volume: "In America people obey the law not merely because they made it but also because they can alter it, if it ever happens to harm them. They obey what they see firstly as a self-imposed evil and secondly as an evil which is always temporary."[58] So compared with what American reviewers had been accustomed to, Tocqueville seemed to be a sincere and fair-minded enthusiast.[59]

One major reason why *Democracy in America* has stood up so well for so long is because we find in Tocqueville a desire for judicious balance. Although he does not come across as neutral—he has too many boldly expressed opinions for that—he is astonishingly nonpartisan. In a letter to an English friend he explains this very clearly:

People want to make me a party man, which I am not. They ascribe to me passions when I have only opinions,—or rather but one passion, the love of freedom and human dignity. All forms of government are in my eyes but means to satisfy this sacred and lawful passion of man. Democratic and aristocratic prejudices are alternately ascribed to me. I should perhaps have had these or those had I been born in another century or in another country; but the accident of my birth has easily enabled me to defend myself against either tendency. I came into the world at the end of a long revolution, which after having destroyed the former state of things had created nothing lasting in its place. Aristocracy was already dead when I began to live, and democracy was not yet in existence. No instinct, therefore, impelled me blindly towards one or the other.[60]

Aside from his sense of balance and proportion, American readers appreciated his clarity, especially notable in those passages where he was most given to generalizations verging on abstraction. His mode of inquiry was not common fare in the United States. He also took pains to define terms, even though key word-concepts like *democracy* and *mores* might be nuanced in diverse ways at different places in his text. At times he seems to address the reader directly and personally, which is especially endearing in a work without an obvious narrative. His topical approach is facilitated by homely analogies, carefully chosen metaphors, and, not incidentally, his moral earnestness, always in evidence.

Early in 1835, just a few weeks following publication of Volume I, Tocqueville wrote to a friend who had read the work carefully but critically. Once again, we cannot help noticing the author's composure, his ability to center his thoughts between ideological or political extremes. His personal preference as an aristocrat, after all, was for constitutional monarchy; but the thrust of his project was future-oriented rather than a matter of contemporary choice. He meant to depict an ideal world as it might take shape in diverse national contexts weighted with historical baggage that could not be casually discarded. As he wrote so poignantly:

To those who have worked out an ideal democracy, a glowing dream, that they believe can easily be realized, I undertook to show that they had covered the picture with false colors; that the democratic government they advocate, if it furnishes real benefits to the men who sustain it, does not have the elevated characteristics that their imagination gives it; that this government, moreover, can be maintained only by means of certain conditions of enlightenment, of private morality, of beliefs that we do not have, and which it is necessary to work to obtain before drawing from them the political consequences.

To men for whom the word *democracy* is synonymous with upheaval, anarchy, spoliation, murders, I tried to show that democracy could manage to govern society while respecting fortunes, recognizing rights, securing liberty, honoring beliefs; that if democratic government developed less than some other governments certain beautiful faculties of the human soul, it had beautiful and grand sides; and that perhaps, after all, the will of God was to diffuse a mediocre happiness on the totality of men, and not to concentrate a large amount of felicity on some and allow only a small number to approach perfection. . . . I please many people of conflicting opinions, not because they understand me, but because they find in my work, by considering it only from a single side, arguments favorable to their passion of the moment.[61]

Within a year, however, as we have noted, Tocqueville received immense acclaim and the greatest distinction his country could bestow. The importance of his work would also receive steadily widening recognition in the United States, not merely from the prestigious men who had received him so cordially and assisted him but from female literati like Catharine Beecher who admired especially the chapters he had devoted to the significant role of American women in the domestic sphere.[62] *Democracy in America* achieved almost instantaneous acceptance as a truly profound inquiry, and would come to be regarded as one of the greatest works of social theory and political science produced during the nineteenth century.

THE RELEVANCE AND LEGACY OF *DEMOCRACY IN AMERICA*

Despite some lapses and misjudgments in the book, readers are more impressed by all the patterns and issues that Tocqueville got right and, above all, his uncanny ability to predict future trends. One authority called this "the grandeur of his prophetic gift."[63] Noting a handful of prescient predictions will suffice. He feared that the dynamics of a democratic society would foster social conformity. By the 1950s an array of thoughtful sociologists and journalists, led by David Riesman's emphasis on "other-directedness" (taking cues from one's peers) in his book *The Lonely Crowd* (1950), would highlight the notable increase in conformity within a paradoxical society that some referred to as a "herd of individuals."[64] Tocqueville also feared, as we have seen, that an excess of individualism would cause Americans to withdraw from civic life, concerning themselves primarily with family and close friends—a trend that we term *privatization*. Among the most extensive commentaries on that development since World War II have been Robert Bellah and others, *Habits of the Heart: Individualism and Commitment in American Life* (1985) and Robert Putnam's widely noticed book *Bowling Alone: The Collapse and Revival of American Community* (2000).

Tocqueville was concerned about what he called "democratic envy" because an egalitarian society made people more competitive. He observed that the appetite for equality encouraged materialism, but instead of satisfying people's acquisitiveness only made them more anxious. From Thorstein Veblen's *Theory of the Leisure Class* (1899) to Vance Packard's best-selling work *The Status Seekers* (1959), critics have called attention to conspicuous consumption and, more recently, to consumerism rocketing out of control. "Keeping up with the Joneses" may be a descriptive cliché, yet it remains more apt than ever. Tocqueville also worried that commercial and industrial property would become overly concentrated in the hands of a few, and thereby diminish democracy. Not many can convincingly dispute the strangling reach of corporate America and the political leverage that it enjoys, ranging from pharmaceutical and insurance companies to news media conglomerates.[65]

Tocqueville warned about the divisiveness of race, referring to the intensifying dispute over slavery. Although he did not directly predict the Civil War that erupted in 1861, he expressed growing concern about the Union's ability to cohere and remain whole because of sectional differences. Even so, he believed that Americans carried their patriotism to absurd extremes. He would not be surprised to see today the proliferation of American flags on private vehicles, mailboxes, athletic uniforms, and in front of residences—displays that are very un-French. In his country the tricolor (national flag) only hangs on public buildings. Though, as has been noted, Tocqueville was genuinely impressed, even *moved* by the Fourth of July celebration and sentiments that he and Beaumont witnessed at Albany in 1831.

Tocqueville lamented that liberty appeared to be a secondary rather than a primary concern for Americans, who almost seemed to take their liberties for granted. Polls have indicated that a majority of Americans continue to accept or approve of the Patriot Act (2003) even though it entails invasions of their privacy and personal freedom. Tocqueville feared that a democracy would not produce "great men," and especially not great leaders; and he predicted that the most able individuals would not seek high office in the civil sphere because private pursuits were more lucrative. Many Americans today are persuaded that he was right, despite some notable exceptions.

His most famous prophecy appeared at the very end of Volume I, when he anticipated that one day the world would be dominated by two great powers that seemed highly unlikely candidates in 1835: the United States and Russia. "Today," he remarked, "two great nations of the earth seem to be advancing toward the same destination from different starting points: the Russians and the Anglo-Americans. Both have grown unobserved and while men's attention has been preoccupied elsewhere, they have climbed up into the leading rank of nations. . . . All other nations appear to have reached almost the upper limits of their natural development and have nothing left to do except preserve what they have, whereas these two nations are growing."[66] Those words would seem amazingly prescient during the cold war (1946–1989) for Tocqueville concluded Volume I with these words: "The point of departure is different, their paths are diverse but each of them seems destined by some secret providential design to hold in their hands the fate of half the world at some date in the future." With that closing piece of futurology, the author's amazing wisdom became a genuine marvel to readers and pundits during the second half of the twentieth century.

In terms of its legacy, as one scholar has observed, "the systematic comparison of two types of society, in order to explain the nature of modernity, became a kind of norm after Tocqueville."[67] The work's reputation has endured, of course, and Tocqueville continues to be quoted from many perspectives and for multiple purposes by statesmen, journalists, and students of public affairs as well as scholars.[68]

His great book remains indispensable for anyone wishing to understand the very nature of democracy in general and its American manifestations in particular. Unlike some "classic" works, *Democracy in America* brilliantly outlives the particular time and circumstances of its composition. It continues to provoke and stimulate thought, perhaps to a greater extent than any other work ever written about the United States, its institutions, and its customs—political, social, and cultural. It supplies us with a heady sense of good fortune concerning our civic heritage, even as it admonishes us to remain ever watchful about the ways in which that legacy might be jeopardized by underlying perils that remain as inherent obstacles to the fulfillment of democracy under changing circumstances that even Tocqueville himself could not have envisioned.

NOTES

[1] See André Jardin, *Tocqueville: A Biography* (New York: Farrar, Straus and Giroux, 1988), chs. 1–3.

[2] Ibid., ch. 4; Barbara Allen, *Tocqueville, Covenant, and the Democratic Revolution: Harmonizing Earth with Heaven* (Lanham, Md.: Rowman & Littlefield, 2005).

[3] Matthew Mancini, *Alexis de Tocqueville and American Intellectuals from His Time to Ours* (Lanham, Md.: Rowman & Littlefield, 2006), 39–40.

[4] George Wilson Pierson, *Tocqueville and Beaumont in America* (New York: Oxford University Press, 1938), 733–34.

[5] Jardin, *Tocqueville*, 90–92.

[6] Quoted in ibid., 90.

[7] Quoted in ibid., 94.

[8] See Johann N. Neem, "Squaring the Circle: The Multiple Purposes of Civil Society in Tocqueville's *Democracy in America*," *Tocqueville Review* 27, no. 1 (2006): 99–121.

[9] See Pierson, *Tocqueville and Beaumont in America*, 517–23.

[10] Unpublished letter to Ernest de Chabrol, July 16, 1831, quoted in Jardin, *Tocqueville*, 118.

[11] Quoted in Pierson, *Tocqueville and Beaumont in America*, 68, 80–81.

[12] See ibid., chs. 18–19.

[13] Alexis de Tocqueville, *Democracy in America and Two Essays on America*, ed. Isaac Kramnick (New York: Penguin Books, 2003), 875–927.

[14] See John F. Sears, *Sacred Places: American Tourist Attractions in the Nineteenth Century* (Amherst: University of Massachusetts Press, 1989), 12–30.

[15] Pierson, *Tocqueville and Beaumont in America*, ch. 24.

[16] Ibid., chs. 25 and 26.

[17] Ibid., chs. 50 and 51.

[18] Quoted in Larry Siedentop, *Tocqueville* (Oxford: Oxford University Press, 1994),68.

[19] Seymour Drescher, "More Than America: Comparison and Synthesis in *Democracy in America*," in *Reconsidering Tocqueville's* Democracy in America, ed. Abraham S. Eisenstadt, 77–93 (New Brunswick, N.J.: Rutgers University Press, 1988); Cushing Strout, "Tocqueville's Duality: Describing America and Thinking of Europe," *American Quarterly* 21 (Spring 1969): 87–99.

[20] Both quotations are from John Stone and Stephen Mennell, eds., *Alexis de Tocqueville: On Democracy, Revolution and Society* (Chicago: University of Chicago Press, 1980), 18, 26.

[21] See Pierson, *Tocqueville and Beaumont in America*, 724.

[22] Tocqueville, *Democracy in America* (ETR translation, Vol. I, Pt. 2, ch. 7, p. 74 in this volume).

[23] Ibid., p. 38.

[24] Tocqueville, *Democracy in America*, ed. Isaac Kramnick (New York: Penguin Books, 2003), 335–36.

[25] Roger Boesche, "Why Did Tocqueville Think a Successful Revolution Was Impossible?" in *Liberty, Equality, Democracy*, ed. Eduardo Nolla (New York: New York University Press, 1992), 179–80.

[26] See Jack Lively, *The Social and Political Thought of Alexis de Tocqueville* (Oxford: Clarendon Press, 1965), 49–50; Seymour Drescher, *Dilemmas of Democracy: Tocqueville and Modernization* (Pittsburgh: University of Pittsburgh Press, 1968), 30–31; Pierson, *Tocqueville and Beaumont in America*, 746–47.

[27] Quoted in James T. Schleifer, *The Making of Tocqueville's* Democracy in America (Chapel Hill: University of North Carolina Press, 1980), 263.

[28] Tocqueville, *Democracy in America* (ETR translation, p. 37 below).

[29] Quoted in Pierson, *Tocqueville and Beaumont in America*, 752.

[30]Both quotations are from S. Karin Amos, *Alexis de Tocqueville and the American National Identity* (Frankfurt: Peter Lang, 1995), 42–43, 108.

[31]Tocqueville, *Democracy in America* (ETR translation, Preface to Vol. II, pp. 96–97 below).

[32]Ibid, Vol. I, Pt. 2, ch. 9, p. 90 below.

[33]Henry Reeve, *Royal and Republican France* (London: Longmans, Green and Co., 1872), II, 85.

[34]Cheryl B. Welch, *De Tocqueville* (Oxford: Oxford University Press, 2001), 51; John Stuart Mill, *Essays on Politics and Society*, ed. J. M. Robson (Toronto: University of Toronto Press, 1977), 50–90, 155–200, vol. 18 in *Collected Works of John Stuart Mill.*

[35]For the particular influence of Johann Gottfried Herder on this type of thinking, see Isaiah Berlin, "Herder and the Enlightenment," in *Vico and Herder: Two Studies in the History of Ideas* (London: Hogarth Press, 1976), esp. 148–50, 174–86, 188–94, 206–13.

[36]See Rupert Wilkinson, *The Pursuit of American Character* (New York: Harper & Row, 1988), index under Tocqueville; Thomas L. Hartshorne, *The Distorted Image: Changing Conceptions of the American Character since Turner* (Cleveland: Press of Case Western Reserve University, 1968); Rupert Wilkinson, ed., *American Social Character: Modern Interpretations* (New York: Harper & Row, 1992); Michael McGiffert, ed., *The Character of Americans: A Book of Readings* (Homewood, Ill.: Dorsey Press, 1964).

[37]See for context Reginald Horsman, *Race and Manifest Destiny: The Origins of American Racial Anglo-Saxonism* (Cambridge, Mass.: Harvard University Press, 1981); Matthew Frye Jacobson, *Whiteness of a Different Color: European Immigrants and the Alchemy of Race* (Cambridge, Mass.: Harvard University Press, 1998).

[38]See Welch, *De Tocqueville*, 78.

[39]Tocqueville, *Democracy in America* (see ETR translation, Vol. I, Pt. 1, ch. 2, p. 53 below).

[40]Ibid., Vol. II, Pt. 4, ch. 34, p. 168 below.

[41]See Tocqueville, *Democracy in America*, 326, 819; J. P. Mayer, *Alexis de Tocqueville: A Biographical Essay in Political Science* (New York: Viking, 1940), 61.

[42]Tocqueville's belief that a higher law of universal justice should supersede a law made by a tyrannical majority notably anticipates the views of Henry David Thoreau and Martin Luther King Jr. See Tocqueville, *Democracy in America* (ETR translation, Vol. I, Pt. 2, ch. 7, pp. 69, 70, 73 below).

[43]See Michael Schudson, *Discovering the News: A Social History of American Newspapers* (New York: Basic Books, 1978), ch. 1; Kenneth Cmiel, *Democratic Eloquence: The Fight over Popular Speech in Nineteenth-Century America* (Berkeley: University of California Press, 1990), ch. 2; Paul Starr, *The Creation of the Media: Political Origins of Modern Communications* (New York: Basic Books, 2004), chs. 3 and 4. See Tocqueville, *Democracy in America* (ETR translation, Vol. I, Pt. 2, ch. 7, p. 76).

[44]Tocqueville to Louis de Kergorlay, June 29, 1831, in Alexis de Tocqueville, *Selected Letters on Politics and Society*, ed. Roger Boesche (Berkeley: University of California Press, 1985), 46.

[45]Quoted in Drescher, *Dilemmas of Democracy*, 260 n. 4.

[46]Pierson, *Tocqueville and Beaumont in America*, 731.

[47]See Tocqueville, *Democracy in America*, 60–64.

[48]See Pierson, *Tocqueville and Beaumont in America*, 126–28, 158–59.

[49]See Sean Wilentz, *The Rise of American Democracy: Jefferson to Lincoln* (New York: W. W. Norton, 2005), 205–16, 327, 392–401.

[50]Sean Wilentz, "Many Democracies: On Tocqueville and Jacksonian America," in Eisenstadt, ed., *Reconsidering Tocqueville's* Democracy in America, 208–9. See also Tocqueville, *Democracy in America*, 65–66; and see Edward Pessen, *Riches, Class, and Power before the Civil War* (Lexington, Mass.: D. C. Heath, 1973), 1–3, 77–78, 128–38.

[51] See Jean-Claude Lamberti, "Two Ways of Conceiving the Republic," in *Interpreting Tocqueville's* Democracy in America, ed. Ken Masugi (Lanham, Md.: Rowman and Littlefield, 1991), 3–26.

[52] Compare Seymour Drescher, "Tocqueville's Two *Démocraties*," *Journal of the History of Ideas* 25 (April 1964): 1–15, and James T. Schleifer, *The Making of Tocqueville's* Democracy in America, 2nd ed. (Indianapolis: Liberty Fund, 2000), 354–68.

[53] Tocqueville, *Democracy in America* (ETR translation, Vol. II, Pt. 2, ch. 21, p. 127 below).

[54] See Hugh Brogan, *Alexis de Tocqueville: A Life* (New Haven, Conn.: Yale University Press, 2007), 450–53, 456.

[55] See Siedentop, *Tocqueville*, 91.

[56] The concept actually had its genesis in Volume I, when Tocqueville wrote, "Each man takes pride in the nation, the successes it gains seem his own work, and he becomes elated." See Welch, *De Tocqueville*, 91.

[57] See Tocqueville, *Democracy in America*, 277.

[58] Ibid., 282.

[59] See Henry Steele Commager, ed., *America in Perspective: The United States through Foreign Eyes* (New York: Random House, 1947); Jane Mesick, *The English Traveller in America, 1785–1835* (Westport, Conn.: Greenwood Press, 1970); Allan Nevins, ed., *America through British Eyes* (New York: Oxford University Press, 1948); Henry T. Tuckerman, *America and Her Commentators* (New York: Scribner's, 1864).

[60] Quoted in Reeve, *Royal and Republican France*, II, 89.

[61] Tocqueville to Eugene Stoffels, February 21, 1835, in Boesche, ed., *Selected Letters on Politics and Society*, 98–100.

[62] See Mancini, *Alexis de Tocqueville and American Intellectuals*, 45–46.

[63] Mayer, *Alexis de Tocqueville: A Biographical Essay in Political Science*, 63.

[64] See also Sloan Wilson, *The Man in the Gray Flannel Suit* (New York: Simon & Schuster, 1955).

[65] See Susan J. Matt, *Keeping Up with the Joneses: Envy in American Consumer Society, 1890–1930* (Philadelphia: University of Pennsylvania Press, 2003); Herbert I. Schiller, *Culture, Inc.: The Corporate Takeover of Public Expression* (New York: Oxford University Press, 1989).

[66] Tocqueville, *Democracy in America*, 484.

[67] Siedentop, *Tocqueville*, 142.

[68] See Michael Kammen, *Alexis de Tocqueville and* Democracy in America (Washington, D.C.: Library of Congress, 1998), 34–36.

PART TWO

Democracy in America

Volume I

AUTHOR'S INTRODUCTION

Of all the novel features that drew my attention during my stay in the United States, the most striking was the equality of conditions. The profound influence of this fact on social affairs was not difficult to discern: it gives a particular direction to public life and a distinctive aspect to laws, new maxims to those who govern, and certain distinctive customs to the governed.

I soon recognized that the influence of equality extends far beyond political custom and law, and that it has no less sway over civil society than over government; it forms opinions, gives rise to feelings, promotes habits, and alters those things it does not actually produce.

Accordingly, from my study of American society, it became increasingly apparent that the condition of equality gave rise to every other detail; it was before me constantly, the central point to which all my observations returned.

When I reflected on our own hemisphere, it seemed to me that I detect something analogous to the scene I found in the New World. The equality of stations, although not yet at the extreme limits to be found in the United States, is gaining ground every day; and the same movement toward democracy that prevails in American society seemed to me to be rapidly growing in strength.

It was then I conceived the idea for this book.

A great democratic revolution is underway: everyone sees it, but not everyone judges it in the same manner. Some consider it as a novelty, a fad they think they will be able to check; others see it as something unstoppable, because to them it is the most continuous, the oldest, and the most permanent revolution known to history. [. . .]

The gradual spread of conditions of equality is ordained in several respects: it is universal, it is lasting, it always eludes the control of authority; events, as well as individuals all contribute to its spread.

Would it be wise to think that a social movement that has spread so far could be halted by the efforts of a single generation? Does anyone believe that after having destroyed feudalism and defeated kings, democracy will withdraw in the face of merchants and the wealthy? Will it subside now that it has grown so strong and its enemies so weak?

What is next? No one can say; for already we lack any basis for comparison; conditions today are more equal among Christian peoples than they have ever been, in any time or any country in the world; the very enormity of what has already taken place prevents our predicting what may yet occur.

This entire work has been written under the spell of a kind of religious terror in the soul of the author, a terror produced by the sight of an irresistible revolution that has been underway for so many centuries, overcoming every obstacle, and that today is proceeding amid all the destruction it has caused.

God need not speak to us directly for us to grasp the clear signs of his will; we need only examine the usual course of nature and the continuous flow of events; I know, without a word from the Creator, that the stars in outer space are following the arc traced by His fingers.

If long observation and honest reflection has led people today to acknowledge that the gradual and progressive expansion of equality is both the past and future of their history, this alone would give one a sense of its expansion as having been blessed by the great Creator. To wish to halt democracy seems then like a struggle against God himself, and nations can do nothing other than accept the social order imposed on them by Providence.

It seems to me that Christian nations today offer a frightening spectacle; the current carrying them is already too strong to stop, and yet not so fast that they despair of controlling it; their fate is still in their hands but will soon have slipped away.

To instruct democracy, if possible to revive its beliefs, purify its morals, regulate its movements; gradually to substitute experience for inexperience, knowledge of true interests for blind instincts; adapt government to time and place and modify it according to the circumstances of the people: of all the tasks required of the leaders of our day who govern society, these are foremost.

A new political science is required for an entirely new world.

But we are not addressing these issues; finding ourselves in the middle of a fast-flowing river, we stubbornly focus on some debris spotted on the banks, while the current that sweeps us away pushes us ever closer to the abyss.

Nowhere in Europe has the great social revolution that I have just described made more progress than amongst ourselves; but here it has developed at random.

Heads of state never thought to plan for this; it has occurred without their knowledge, or in spite of them. The most powerful classes, the most intelligent and most moral elements of the country never sought to take hold of it in order to direct it. So democracy was left to its basest instincts; it has grown like fatherless children who raise themselves in the streets of our cities, knowing only the vices and miseries of society. We seemed to ignore its existence until it had unexpectedly seized power. Then everyone submitted to its every whim with servility; it was worshipped as the image of power. When, later, democracy was weakened by its own excess, legislators imprudently decided to destroy it rather than correct and instruct it. Not willing to teach it to govern, they thought only of repudiating it.

The result is that a democratic revolution has taken place in the fabric of society without making any of the changes in laws, ideas, habits, and morals necessary to make the revolution useful. So we have a democracy lacking the means necessary to attenuate its vices and emphasize its natural advantages; and while we now see the evils it has brought, we ignore the benefits it might offer. [. . .]

So now we have abandoned whatever good the old state held, while failing to gain whatever good the current state could offer; we have destroyed an aristocratic society, and, suspended complacently in the middle of the ruins of the old edifice, we seem to intend to remain there forever.

What is happening in the intellectual world is no less deplorable.

Impeded in its advance or thrown without support on its chaotic passions, democracy in France has overturned everything in its way, weakening whatever it did not destroy. We have not seen it take hold of society gradually, the better to establish its power there in peace; rather, it has continued to charge into the tumults and confusion of battle. Animated by the heat of battle, and pushed beyond the natural limits of their own opinions by the opinions and the excesses of their adversaries, people have lost sight of the very object they are seeking and employ a rhetoric that poorly expresses their true feelings and private instincts.

We are forced to witness the bizarre confusion that has emerged from this.

In vain I search my memory to find anything more worthy of sorrow and pity than what passes before our eyes: it seems that the natural link uniting judgment with taste and acts with beliefs has been broken; the agreement that could once be found between men's feelings and ideals seems broken, and one could say that all the laws of moral analogy are broken.

We still meet ardent Christian people whose religious zeal prefers to be fed on the truths of the next life; surely they will be inspired to favor human freedom, the source of all moral greatness. Christianity, which says that all men are equal before God, will not reject the image of citizens equal before the law. However, through a strange confluence of events, religion is momentarily involved with powers that democracy opposes, and frequently it repudiates the very equality it loves, and curses liberty as an enemy, whereas by embracing equality, religion might have redeemed it.

On the side of these religious men, I have met others whose gaze is turned to earth rather than to heaven; partisans of liberty, not only because they see in it the origin of the noblest virtues but especially because they consider it as the source of the greatest good, they sincerely wish to establish its empire and offer men a taste of its fruits; I would expect them to hasten to call upon religion to help them, knowing that one cannot establish a reign of liberty without morality, nor establish morality without faith. However, they have seen religion in the ranks of their enemies and that is enough: some attack religion, others dare not defend it.

In centuries past there have been those, base and evil people, who sanctioned slavery, while those with independent spirits and generous hearts fought in vain to protect human freedom. However, in our time we often meet people, by nature noble and proud, whose opinions are in contradiction to their values and who praise a servility and low status they have never known themselves. Then there are others who speak of liberty as if they were able to sense the holiness and greatness within it, and who noisily claim for humanity rights they have always scorned.

I see some good and even-tempered people whose pure morals, quiet habits, prosperity, and talents naturally place them ahead of those around them. Full of a sincere love for their country, they are ready to make great sacrifices for it: however they are often found to be adversaries of civilization; they confuse its abuses with its benefits, and in their minds the essence of evil is indissolubly united with the new.

Next to these I see others who, in the name of progress, have a materialistic view of man, and seek utility instead of justice, science without belief, and well-being without virtue: these are said to be the champions of modern civilization, and they push ahead insolently, usurping places abandoned by others repulsed by their impropriety.

What have we come to?

Religious men fight liberty, and the friends of liberty attack religions; good and noble minds sanction slavery, and common, servile people hail independence; honest and enlightened citizens are the enemies of all progress, while immoral, unpatriotic men consider themselves apostles of civilization and enlightenment!

Have all ages resembled ours? Have men always beheld, as we do today, a world where nothing makes sense, where virtue is without talent and talent without honor; where love of order is confused with a taste for tyranny, and the holy cult of liberty with scorn for laws; where conscience casts only a faint light on human affairs; where nothing is forbidden, or permitted, nothing is honest or shameful, nothing true or false? [. . .]

There is one country in the world where the great social revolution of which I speak seems to have nearly attained its natural limit; it functions there simply and smoothly, or rather one could say that this country enjoys the results of the democratic revolution experienced in our country without the revolution itself.

The emigrants who settled in America at the beginning of the seventeenth century managed to extract the principle of democracy out of all those opposed to it at the heart of the old European societies, and they transplanted it, alone, on the shores of the New World. There, it was able to grow freely and, undisturbed, to develop laws in step with customs.

It seems to me without any doubt that sooner or later we, like the Americans, will attain conditions of almost complete equality. I am far from concluding that we might ever expect to experience, from a comparable social status, the same political consequences as the Americans. I am far from believing that they have found the only form of government that democracy has to offer; but the fact that the force generating laws and morals is the same in the two countries is reason enough for us to be immensely interested in knowing what it has produced in each of them.

It was not simply to satisfy a perfectly legitimate curiosity that I studied America; I wanted to find lessons there from which we can benefit. One would be sorely mistaken to think that I wished to produce a panegyric: anyone who reads this book will be convinced that that was not at all my intention; nor was it my goal to sanction any form of government in general; I am one of those who believes there is almost never absolute goodness in laws; I have never even claimed to judge whether the social revolution, whose progress seems to me to be unstoppable, would serve humanity well or ill; I have taken the revolution as an accomplished fact or nearly so, and, among those people who have seen it at work in their midst, I have looked for the one example where it has attained its fullest and most undisturbed development, in order to see clearly the natural consequences and to observe, if possible, the means of making it advantageous to men. I confess that in America I saw more than America; I was looking for the face of democracy itself, its penchants, character, prejudices, and passions; I needed to know it, if only in order to learn what we had to hope for or fear from it.

In the first part of this work, I have tried to indicate the direction that democracy, in America, free to follow its inclinations and given full rein to pursue its ideals, has taken in its laws, its imprint on government, and generally in the power that it obtained over commerce. I wished to know the results, both the good and the bad; I have researched the precautions Americans have taken to direct it, and those they have failed to take, and I have tried to discern the principles that allow it to govern society.

In Part II, my intention was to describe the power that equality of conditions exercises in America and the way democracy governs civil society, in its habits, its ideas, and its morals; but I am beginning to feel less enthusiasm for this. Before I could complete the task I had set myself, my work would be of no use. Soon, another writer would be describing for readers the principle features of the American character, and, with a light touch veiling the seriousness of the subject, reveal its true charms in a way I could never do.

I do not know if I have been successful in presenting all that I observed in America, but I am confident of having earnestly wished to do so, and of never intentionally yielding to a need to make facts conform to ideas, rather, always demanding that ideas be submitted to facts. [. . .]

I conclude by acknowledging what many readers will consider the greatest flaw of this work. The book does not come in response to any other writer: it was not my intention to advance or oppose any point of view in this work; I wished only to observe, and if not in a different way from others, perhaps to see farther than they; while they are thinking only about tomorrow, I wished to consider the more distant future.

Part I

CHAPTER 1

America's Beginnings and Their Importance for the Future

A man is born; he spends his early years in obscurity among the pleasures and travails of childhood; he grows up, becomes a young man; the doors of the world open to receive him; he interacts with his contemporaries. It is then you study him for the first time, and you think you detect the emergence of his mature vices and virtues.

If I am not mistaken, that is a great error.

Step back; look at the baby in his mother's arms; see the external world as it is reflected for the first time in the still dim mirror of his mind; contemplate the earliest experiences that strike his senses; listen to the first words that awaken in him the dormant powers of thought; finally, observe the earliest conflicts he endures; only then will you understand the source of the prejudices, habits, and passions that will come to rule his life. In this sense, the mature man is formed in infancy.

Something analogous to this happens with nations. People will always be shaped by their origins. The circumstances that accompany their birth and that contribute to their development influence everything for the rest of their lives.

If it were possible to return to the foundations of societies and examine the earliest historical evidence, I have no doubt that we would discover the primary source of prejudice, habit, dominant passions of everything, in short, all that comprises what we call national character; we would encounter an explanation for usages that, today, appear contrary to prevailing customs; of laws that seem to be in opposition to recognized principles; of incoherent opinions that are encountered here and there in the society, like pieces of broken chain that one can sometimes see hanging from the arches of a ruin, holding nothing. This is how we might explain the destiny of certain peoples,

---

Chapter 1 appeared as Volume I, Part I, Chapter 2 in the original, complete text.

seemingly guided by an unknown power toward an end unknown even to themselves. But until now, the circumstances for such a study were missing; the analytical spirit came to nations only with maturity, and when it finally occurred to them to examine their origins, these were already obscured by time, shrouded by ignorance and pride in legends, the truth hidden from view.

America is the only country where one may still observe the natural and undisturbed development of a society, and where it has been possible to recognize the influence of its origins on the future states.

When Europeans first reached the banks of the New World, the traits of their national character were already formed; each one had a distinct physiognomy; and as they had already reached the degree of civilization that leads men to self-study, they transmitted to us a faithful picture of their attitudes, customs, and laws. The men of the fifteenth century are almost as well known to us as are those of our own day. Thus, America has brought to light what the ignorance and barbarism of earliest times had concealed.

Since men of our day are close enough to the period of the founding of the American societies to know their components in detail, yet far enough from that time to be able to assess what grew from those seeds, we seem destined to look deeper into the history of human events than our predecessors. Providence has granted us a light on the past that our fathers' generation lacked, and has shown us, in the destinies of nations, first causes that were previously hidden.

When, after a careful examination of American history, we study its political and social condition closely, we are left with a deep conviction of one truth: that there is not an opinion, a custom, a law, I might even say not a single event, that cannot be easily explained by first beginnings, by the inception. Anyone who reads this book will find, accordingly, in the present chapter, the seed of all that follows and the key to almost the entire work.

The emigrants who came, at different times, to occupy the land that is the American union today, differed from each other in many respects; their goals were not the same, and their self-government was based on different principles.

However, these people had qualities in common, and they found themselves in very similar circumstances.

Language is perhaps the strongest, and most enduring, bond uniting people. The emigrants spoke the same language, all were children of a single people. Born in a country that had been troubled for centuries by partisan wrangling, and where the factions had been obliged to seek the protection of laws, they had received a harsh political education, and amongst them we have seen the spread of more notions about rights and principles of true liberty than among most of the peoples of Europe. At the time of the earliest migrations, self-government, that fertile seed of free institutions, had already penetrated deeply into English custom, and with it the dogma of the sovereignty of the people reached the very heart of the Tudor monarchy.

I have now said enough on the subject to put the character of Anglo-American civilization in its true light. It is the product (and this fundamental point must be kept in mind at all times) of two clearly distinct elements, elements that in other places have often been in conflict, but that Americans have managed to join together and to combine to marvelous effect.

The founders of New England were both ardent sectarians and enthusiastic innovators. Although tightly bound by narrowly strict religious beliefs, they were free of all prejudice in politics.

From this come two diverse, but not conflicting, trends, the signs of which are apparent everywhere, in custom as well as in law.

Some men sacrifice friends, family, and country to a religious view; one might think them absorbed in the pursuit of this intellectual prize that they have come to purchase at so high a price. However, we find that they seek with almost equal fervor material wealth and spiritual joy, heaven in the next world and liberty and prosperity in this.

In their hands, political principles, laws, and human institutions seem to be malleable things, to be shaped and combined at will.

Before them barriers that had once imprisoned the society in the heart of which they had grown, fall away; the old views, which for centuries had governed the world, disappear; an endless path and limitless opportunities open to them. The human spirit races forward, chasing after them in every direction. However, when it reaches the limits of the political sphere, it comes to a stop; shuddering, it deposits the customs of its most alarming qualities; it disavows all doubt, denies the need to innovate; it refuses even to lift the veil of the sanctuary; it bows respectfully before truths that it accepts without discussion.

In morality, everything is classified, coordinated, foreseen, decided in advance, whereas in politics, everything is in flux, contested, uncertain; in the former, passive, voluntary obedience; in the latter, independence, disdain for experience, and resentment of authority.

Rather than threatening each other, these two tendencies, apparently so different, move in unison and seem to offer mutual support.

CHAPTER 2

Anglo-American Social Conditions

Ordinarily, social conditions are the product of acts, sometimes of laws, and most often a combination of the two; however, once established, they may themselves be regarded as a first cause of most laws, customs, and the ideas that govern the conduct of nations; what it does not actually produce, it modifies.

In order to understand the laws and the attitudes of a people, it is therefore necessary to study their social condition.

THE MOST STRIKING ASPECT OF ANGLO-AMERICAN SOCIAL CONDITION IS THAT IT IS ESSENTIALLY DEMOCRATIC

There are a number of important things to be said about the social conditions of Anglo-Americans, but one is paramount.

The American social condition is eminently democratic. This has been its character since the birth of the colonies and it is even more so today.

As I said in the preceding chapter, a high degree of equality prevailed among the emigrants who came to settle on the coast of New England. In this part of the Union, no germ of aristocracy was able to grow. Influence depended entirely on intellect. People came to respect those whose names symbolized enlightenment and virtue. Some citizens obtained a greater influence over the people in a way that might aptly have been called aristocratic if it had been possible to pass that influence intact from father to son.

This was the case east of the Hudson River; but southwest of this river, and as far south as Florida, everything was different.

Chapter 2 appeared as Volume I, Part I, Chapter 3 in the original, complete text.

In most of the States situated southwest of the Hudson, the English were able to establish large landholdings. Aristocratic principles were imported accompanied by English laws of succession. I have described the circumstances that prevented the establishment of a powerful aristocracy in America. While these circumstances were also present in the region southwest of the Hudson, they were less powerful there than east of the river. In the South, a single man could, with the help of slaves, cultivate a vast expanse of land. And so we see in that part of the continent rich landowners; their position, however, was not truly aristocratic in the European sense of the word because they possessed no privileges and because the culture of slavery meant that they had no tenants, consequently no patronage. Still, the great estates south of the Hudson formed an upper class, one with its own attitudes and values, that generally consolidated political power within its own circle. This was an aristocracy that differed little from the mass of people whose passions and interests it readily embraced, arousing neither love nor hate; in summary, weak and lifeless. It was this class that, in the South, led the insurrection; the American Revolution owes its great leaders to this class.

At that time, the entire society was in upheaval; the people in whose name the war was fought and who had become a powerful force developed a desire to act for itself; democratic instincts were awakened; after breaking the yoke of the mother country, a taste for independence had grown: individual influences were felt less and less; laws and customs began to move together toward the same end.

The final step to equality involved the law of inheritance.

I am surprised that both ancient and modern authors have attributed so little importance to the role of laws of inheritance in the course of human affairs. While it is true that these laws belong to the civil sphere, they should be placed in the front rank of all political institutions for they are incredibly influential on the social condition of a nation, of which political laws are simply the expression. They also have a sure and uniform impact on society; in a way, these laws seize control over generations to come. Through them, one person may be armed with an almost divine power over the future of his contemporaries. With a single act, laws of succession affecting all citizens are enacted and the legislation endures for centuries; once set in motion, it remains untouched; the machine runs by itself and is self-guided toward a predetermined end. Constituted in a certain way, it combines and concentrates first propriety and eventually actual power in a single individual; it allows a sort of aristocracy to spring from the soil.

Guided by other principles and launched on a different path, it moves even more quickly; it divides, shares, and spreads wealth and power, and at times the speed of its progress is frightening; with no hope of ever halting the advance, an attempt is made to put obstacles and difficulties in its path; desperate attempts are made to balance its influence. Such efforts are useless. It crushes, or shatters anything it encounters in its path, it rises and falls on the ground endlessly, until all that remains in sight is the shifting and impalpable dust upon which democracy rests.

When the laws of inheritance allow, or more accurately mandate, the equal division of property among all the children, the effects are twofold: it is important to distinguish between them carefully, despite the fact that they tend to the same end.

Owing to the laws on inheritance, the death of every landowner leads to a complete turnover of property; not only do the assets change owners, but the nature of the property changes also; it is broken into increasingly smaller fractions.

That is the direct and to some extent material effect of the law. In countries where legislation establishes equal shares, all assets, and especially property, are permanently shrinking. Nevertheless, if the law were allowed to run its course, the effect of this legislation would be felt only over a long time; for provided that a family consisted of no more than two children (and the average family, in a country like France, is said to be only three), these children, sharing the fortunes of both parents, would be no poorer than each of them individually.

However, the law of equal shares is not only felt in regard to future assets; it affects the minds of the landowners for whom this is an emotional issue. These indirect results quickly destroy large fortunes and particularly large properties.

In nations where the law of inheritance is based upon the right of primogeniture, estates of land usually pass from generation to generation without division. The result is that the identity of the family is expressed through the land. The family represents land and the land represents the family; its name, origins, glory, power, and virtue are perpetuated. Land is permanent evidence of the past and a precious guarantee of its future existence.

When the law of inheritance establishes equal shares, the intimate connection that existed between the family and preservation of its land is destroyed; land ceases to represent the family; when after one or two generations subdivision is unavoidable, it is obvious that the holdings will continue to shrink and ultimately disappear altogether. When a large landowner has few sons, they may, if they are lucky, hope to be no less rich than their parent, but not to possess equal property; their wealth will necessarily consist of elements other than the parent's.

Now, when you remove the sentimental value, memory, pride, and the ambition to preserve the land, you may be sure that sooner or later it will be sold, for there is a strong financial incentive to sell, as real estate assets produce more interest than others, and more readily satisfy short-term desires.

Once divided, large landholdings cannot be reestablished; the small landowner earns a greater profit from his field, relatively speaking, than the large landowner does from his; the former sells at a much higher price than the latter. Hence, the economic calculations that lead a rich man to sell a large property work even more effectively against the re-creation of large properties through the purchase of small ones.

What we call a sense of family is often based on an illusion of individual self-interest. The individual wishes to perpetuate himself, to find a kind of immortality in his great-grandchildren. When the sense of family ends, individual self-interest returns. Since the family exists only in the mind as a vague concept, indeterminate and uncertain, one's focus is on the convenience of the present; his concern is for the establishment of the next generation only, nothing more.

There is no motivation to perpetuate the family, or rather one hopes to perpetuate it through something other than property.

The laws of inheritance not only make it difficult for families to keep the lands intact, they remove the desire to try, and in a way lead families to participate in their own demise.

The law of equal inheritance works in two ways; by acting upon objects, it acts upon individuals; and in acting on individuals, it affects objects.

In both ways, the law manages to strike a blow at land ownership and to make families disappear as quickly as their fortunes.

As French people of the nineteenth century who daily witness the political and social changes brought by laws of succession, it is certainly not for us to question the power of the laws. We see what is happening every day in our country, the walls of our homes overturned and the enclosures of our fields destroyed. But if the law of inheritance has already accomplished a great deal here, there is much more to be done. Our memories, our attitudes, and our habits present a powerful opposition to it.

In the United States, this undoing is almost complete. There, it is possible to examine the principal effects.

English law on the transmission of property was abolished in almost all the States at the time of the Revolution.

The law of entail was modified in such a manner as to leave almost no restraint upon the free sale of property.

Once the first generation had passed away, the land started to be divided. Over time, the process gathered speed. Today, scarcely sixty years later, society has changed almost beyond recognition; the families of large landowners have almost all been absorbed into the general population. In New York State, where there were once a great many estates, two remain, barely surviving above the abyss that awaits them. Today the sons of these wealthy citizens are merchants, lawyers, doctors. Most have dropped into total obscurity. The last traces of rank and hereditary distinctions are almost gone; leveled everywhere by the law of inheritance.

This does not mean that in the United States, as elsewhere, there are no rich people; I don't know of any country, in fact, where the love of money occupies such a large place in the hearts of men, and where people profess a deeper scorn for the theory of a permanent equality of wealth. But fate works there at an incredible rate, and experience teaches that it is rare to see two generations in a row favored by fortune.

This picture, however subjective one might think it, still gives only a partial idea of what is happening in the new states of the West and Southwest.

At the end of the last century, bold explorers began penetrating the valleys of the Mississippi. It was as though America had been discovered for a second time; soon most emigration was occurring there; unknown communities sprang suddenly out of the desert. States whose names did not even exist just a few years earlier took their place in the heart of the American Union. In the West, democracy was seen to reach the ultimate development. In those states, improvised in some respects at random, inhabitants have occupied their land only since yesterday. They hardly know one another and all are ignorant of the history of their closest neighbors. In this part of the American continent, where any sort of natural aristocracy based on talent and virtue is lacking, one does not feel the influence of men of great renown and wealth. There, no one has authority based on respect earned through a life entirely spent in good works. The new states in the West have the people; they do not yet have communities.

But it is not only fortunes that are equal in America; to some extent, equality extends even to intellect.

I do not think that there is a country in the world where, relative to the population, so few are either ignorant or well educated than in America.

Primary instruction is available to everyone; higher education is available to almost no one.

This is easily explained, and is, in fact, the inevitable result of what I have argued above.

Almost all Americans live in comfort and can readily acquire the first elements of human knowledge.

In America, there are few rich people. Most Americans need a profession and every profession demands an apprenticeship. Americans cannot, therefore, afford to give more than the first few years of life to cultivating general intelligence. At fifteen years, they begin a career; and so their education generally ends at the time when ours begins. If education continues beyond that, it is directed toward a lucrative, specialized field. Science is learned along with a trade and only that which has immediate application and obvious utility.

In America, most rich people were first poor; most men of leisure were, in their youth, hard-working. Consequently, at the time when one might have an appetite for learning, there is no time to pursue it, and when one has the time for the pursuit of learning, the desire is gone.

There is not in America any class with the hereditary comfort and leisure to pass along the inclination for intellectual pursuits, or that values the work of the mind.

Hence, the desire to pursue such work is lacking as well as the ability to do so.

In the area of human knowledge, a certain mediocrity has been established. The intellects of some rise, and of others decline, to this level.

In this way large numbers of people are assembled who have about the same number of ideas on matters of religion, history, science, political economy, legislation, and government.

Intellectual inequality comes directly from God, and men will never be able to change that.

However, though men's minds may be unequally endowed by their Creator, the opportunities available to them are equal.

And so in America today the aristocratic element, weak from the very beginning, is, if not destroyed, so weakened that it is difficult for it to exercise any influence whatsoever over events.

Time, circumstances, and laws have made the democratic element, on the contrary, not only preponderant, but, in a manner of speaking, unique. No trace of family or class influence remains; often it is impossible to detect even any lasting personal influence.

In its social condition, America thus represents a very strange phenomenon. Men there are more equal in fortune and intelligence, in other words in strength, than anywhere in the world and more than they have been during any century in history.

POLITICAL CONSEQUENCES OF ANGLO-AMERICAN SOCIAL CONDITIONS

The political consequences of these social conditions are obvious.

It is impossible to imagine that equality will not penetrate the political sphere as it has others. It would be unlikely for a people to remain forever unequal in one sphere, while equal in all others; they will, at some point, attain equality in all.

I know only two ways of making equality work in the political arena; rights must be given to everyone, or to none.

When a nation has reached the social condition of Anglo-Americans, it is thus very difficult to imagine some middle ground between the sovereignty of all and the absolute power of one.

We should not pretend that the social condition I have just described does not lend itself to both of these two conclusions.

There is in fact a legitimate and manly passion for equality that excites in men a desire for all to be strong and worthy. This passion tends to lift the weak to the level of the strong; but there is also in the human heart a taste for perverse equality, which makes weak men wish to see the strong brought to their level and which leads them to prefer equality in servitude to inequality in freedom. This is not because people whose social condition is democratic scorn liberty; on the contrary, they have an instinctive taste for it. For them equality, not liberty, is the principal and constant objective; they grope for liberty in fits and starts and, failing, resign themselves; but without equality, nothing satisfies them, and they would rather perish than lose that.

Another part of this is that when citizens are almost all equal, it becomes difficult for them to defend their independence from the aggressions of authority. As no one is powerful enough by himself to resist, only the combined force of all can guarantee liberty. That combination cannot always be found.

The political consequences of a condition of social equality for the people are therefore very great; these consequences can be widely different, but they all derive from the same fact.

The first citizens to be subject to the risks I have described, Anglo-Americans have had the good fortune to avoid absolute power. Circumstances, origins, talents, and especially attitudes have enabled them to establish and maintain the sovereignty of the people.

CHAPTER 3

The Principle of the Sovereignty of the People in America

Anyone who wishes to speak about political laws in the United States must begin with the belief in the principle of the sovereignty of the people.

This principle, which can be found to some degree at the heart of almost all human institutions, is normally deeply buried. It is understood though never acknowledged, and when it is occasionally and momentarily brought to light, it is hastily shoved back into its shadowy sanctuary.

The "national will" is one of those phrases that schemers of every era and despots of every age have most abused. Some think it is expressed in the compliance bought by agents of power; others see it in the votes of a self-interested or fearful minority; there are even some who have seen it expressed by the people's silence, who thought their *right* to rule derived from the *fact* that others obeyed.

In America, the principle of popular sovereignty is neither hidden nor impotent, as it is in some nations; it is recognized in values,

---

Chapter 3 appeared as Volume I, Part I, Chapter 4 in the original, complete text.

heralded in laws; it expands with liberty and moves unencumbered to its ultimate fulfillment.

If there is one country in the world where one can hope to appreciate the full value of the principle of popular sovereignty, and to study both the benefits and dangers of applying it in the affairs of society, surely that country is America.

As I have noted previously, the principle of popular sovereignty has been, from the very beginning, one of the founding principles of most of the English colonies in America.

However, at that time it lacked the ability to dominate the governing of society that it has today.

Two obstacles impeded its progress, one external, the other internal.

Popular sovereignty could not be clearly established by law because the colonies were still obliged to obey the mother country; so it was concealed in the provincial assemblies and especially in the township. There it secretly expanded.

Moreover, American society at that time was not yet prepared to adopt the principle of popular sovereignty in all of its ramifications. As I described in the preceding chapter, the intellectuals in New England and the wealthy living south of the Hudson had for some time exerted a quasi-aristocratic influence which had the effect of limiting the number of people who actually governed. This was still long before the election of public officials and the extension of voting rights to all citizens. The right to vote was limited in all the colonies and depended upon a property requirement. The requirement was very small in the North, substantially greater in the South.

Then the American Revolution began. Belief in the sovereignty of the people emerged from the local arena and took hold in government: all classes endorsed it; battles were fought and won in its name; it became the law of laws.

Another change took place within society, almost as quickly. The law of inheritance broke free of local influences.

Once this combined effect of law and the revolution began to be noticed by everyone, the battle was won in favor of democracy. Power was effectively in the people's hands. It was no longer possible to fight it. Upper classes had submitted without a murmur and without a fight to an evil they considered inevitable. They experienced what happens whenever power falls: self-interest appeared in their ranks. As it was impossible to retake power from the hands of the people, and as no one despised the mob enough to wish to confront it, they thought only of winning its approval at any cost. In most cases, people supported laws that were against their own interests. Thus the upper classes did nothing to excite the anger of the people against them; instead, they themselves hastened the victory of the new order. As strange as it may seem, democracy seemed most irresistible where aristocracy had the deepest roots.

The State of Maryland, founded by Old World nobility, was first to proclaim universal suffrage and introduced the most democratic practices into its government.

It is clear that once people begin to reform restrictions on suffrage, it will be only a matter of time before they are abolished entirely. That is one of the most invariable of laws governing society. As soon as the barriers to voting rights are lowered, the pressure grows to lower them further; after each new concession, the strength of democracy grows and its needs increase with its expanding power. The demands of those denied electoral rights grow as the number of those with voting rights grows. The exception ultimately becomes the rule; concessions are constantly being made, stopping only when universal suffrage is won.

Today, the principle of the sovereignty of the people has achieved every practical application imaginable. It has freed itself of all the make-believe that was carefully erected around it in other places; it has appeared in every possible shape, according to the circumstances. Sometimes the people as a whole make the laws, as in Athens; sometimes their deputies, elected through universal suffrage, represent them, acting in their name and under their immediate supervision.

In some countries authority rests outside the society at large but acts upon it and forcibly moves it in a certain direction.

In others, power is divided, residing both inside and outside society. This is not the case in the United States: there society acts by and on itself. All power is under its control; you cannot meet anyone who would even dare imagine, much less express, the thought of looking for power anywhere else. The people participate in the writing of laws through their choice of legislators and in the enactment of them through the election of officials with executive authority; one can say that the people govern themselves, as the executive authority is weak and limited and highly aware of its popular roots and subject to the popular mandate. The people rule in the American political realm as God rules the universe. The people are the end-all and be-all; everything is derived from and absorbed by the people.

CHAPTER 4

The Need to Examine What Happens in the States before Discussing the Federal Government

In the following chapter I intend to study the American form of government established on the principle of popular sovereignty; how it functions, its problems, its advantages, and its risks.

One difficulty arises right away: the United States has a complex Constitution; two distinct systems are involved, and, in a manner of speaking, one is contained inside the other; two completely separate and almost independent governments are found; one, more common and less restricted to address day-to-day issues of society, while the other is more circumscribed and addresses certain exceptional concerns of a general nature. In a word, there are twenty-four small sovereign nations that together form the Union as a whole.

If we were to study the Union before the individual states we would find our path strewn with obstacles. The structure of the federal government in the United States came last; it was a simple modification of the republic, a resumption of political principles that were widespread in the society preceding it and that existed independently. The federal government, moreover, as I have just said is, in a word, exceptional; state government is the local authority. Any attempt to describe the whole of such a picture before having presented the parts would necessarily lead to vagueness and repetition.

The grand political principles that govern American society today originated and developed in the *state*; of that there is no doubt. Therefore an understanding of the state is the key to understanding the whole.

The states that comprise the American Union today all look the same in terms of their institutions' external appearance. The administrative or political life is concentrated in three levels of activity, comparable to the various nerve centers that control the movements of the human body.

The first level is the township, then the county, and finally the state. [. . .]

Chapter 4 appeared as Volume I, Part I, Chapter 5 in the original, complete text.

THE SPIRIT OF THE TOWNSHIP
IN NEW ENGLAND

Not only do local institutions exist in America, but these are animated and supported by a clear sense of community.

Townships throughout New England enjoy two advantages that together animate a lively interest among men: independence and power. Local government operates within a narrowly defined sphere of influence, but within that sphere, it moves freely. It is this autonomy alone that gives the township its importance; on the basis of population and size its influence would be slight.

It is necessary to recognize that men's affections are generally directed to the center of power. We do not see love of country enduring for long after a nation is conquered. The inhabitant of New England is attached to his township not so much because he was born there but because in the township he sees himself belonging to a strong and free association that merits the effort he makes to lead it.

In Europe, governments themselves often lament the absence of a sense of community, which most people would agree is a large part of public order and tranquility; but they do not know how to instill it. They are afraid that creating strong and independent townships would divide power over society and expose the state to anarchy. But, remove the power and independence from the township and you are left not with citizens but administrative units.

There is another important fact to notice: the New England township is so constituted that it serves as the center of a spirited affection, and at the same time there is nothing about it to excite passionate ambition in the human heart.

County officials are not elected and their authority is limited. The State itself has only a secondary importance; its existence is obscure and quiet. There are few men who would agree to disrupt their lives for an administrative post, leaving the center of their own interests.

The federal government confers power and glory on those who govern, but there are few men who are given that chance to shape their own destinies. The Presidency is a high office to which one can aspire only at an advanced age; and it is largely by chance that anyone attains other high level federal offices, and only after earning reknown pursuing some other career. It is not attained through lifelong ambition for the position. It is in the township, at the center of the ordinary activities of life, that the desire for esteem grows, the need for actual achievement, the taste for power and activity; these passions, so often troubling to society, change character when they can be expressed close to home and in some sense within the family.

Look how adroitly power in the American townships has been *scattered*, so to speak, in order to involve more people in public affairs. Aside from the electors who are called from time to time to vote on government business, notice how many different jobs there are, how many magistrates, all of whom, within their areas of responsibility, are representatives of the powerful body in whose name they serve. Many men benefit from and involve themselves in the leadership of the town.

In the American system of sharing municipal authority among a large number of citizens, there is no fear of these multiple township responsibilities. In the United States it is accurate to think of love of country as a kind of religion in which men practice certain rituals.

Community life is thus felt in everything; it is manifest every day in the fulfillment of some duty or the exercise of some right. Political activity exerts a pressure that is constant but calm, that stirs up without disturbing.

Americans attach themselves to the city for the same reason that mountain people love their hills. For them, the fatherland has pronounced and characteristic features; it has more of a face than elsewhere. [. . .]

POLITICAL EFFECTS OF ADMINISTRATIVE DECENTRALIZATION IN THE UNITED STATES

Centralization is a word one hears repeated constantly today, but, generally speaking, no one is very clear about what it means.

There are, however, two very distinct kinds of centralization, and it is important to recognize them.

Some issues affect a nation as a whole, such as the formation of general laws and foreign affairs.

Other issues belong more to specific sectors, such as the affairs of townships.

I will call the concentration in one place or person the power to direct issues of the first type, governmental centralization.

The same concentration of power to direct issues of the second type is what I will call administrative centralization.

There are areas in which these two types of centralization become indistinguishable. But by sorting the items that belong, on the whole, more specifically in one area or the other, these distinctions become clear.

We know that when governmental centralization is joined to administrative centralization, it is much more powerful. This is how people become used to a total and permanent submission of their own will; they obey, not only once or in one thing, but always and in everything. Power subdues them by force, and controls their habits; it isolates them and holds them one by one in the common mass.

These two kinds of centralization are mutually supportive, each drawn to the other; I cannot, however, believe that they are inseparable.

France, under Louis XIV, experienced the greatest concentration of governmental authority imaginable, for it was the same individual who made general laws and interpreted them, represented France abroad, and acted in his own name. I am the State, he proclaimed, quite accurately.

However, under Louis XIV, there was much less administrative centralization than in our own day.

Today, we see one power, England, that has taken governmental centralization to a very high level; the State there seems to move as a single entity; it binds an immense mass to its bidding and joining all its forces, employs its power wherever it wishes.

England, which has done such great things for the last fifty years, does not have administrative centralization.

It is impossible for me to imagine that a nation could live or, more importantly, prosper without a strong central government.

However, I believe that administrative centralization serves only to weaken the people who submit to it, for it tends continually to lower their civic spirit. It is true that administrative centralization manages to bring together at one time and in one place all the available forces of the state, but it damages the ability to sustain its strength. It prevails in battle, but it diminishes power in the long term. It can indeed contribute admirably to the momentary greatness of one man, but not at all in the permanent prosperity of a people. [. . .]

We have seen that the United States has no centralized administration. There is almost no trace of hierarchy. I believe that decentralization has reached a degree that no European nation could tolerate comfortably, and that even in America has had some troubling results. However, governmental centralization in the United States is quite advanced. It would be easy to demonstrate that national power in America is more concentrated than it ever was in the former monarchies of

Europe. Not only is there but a single body making laws in each state; not only is there a single authority that is able to build a political base around itself; but in general, unification of the populous district or county assemblies has been prevented out of a fear that these assemblies would be tempted to go beyond their administrative functions and interfere with the working of government. In America there is no authority that can check the legislature of each state. Nothing is capable of blocking its path, neither privileges, local immunity, or personal influence; not even the authority of reason, for it represents the majority that claims to be the sole voice of reason. There is, therefore, nothing to limit its activity other than its own will. Beside it, and in its hands, stands the representative of the executive power, to compel, with the aid of physical force, the obedience of dissidents.

Weakness appears only in certain details of governmental activity.

The American republics have no permanent armed forces with which to repress minorities, but the minorities have not, as yet, had reason to appeal to arms and so far the need for an army has not been felt. Ordinarily, the state calls on the officials of the township or county to manage the affairs of citizens. Thus, for example, in New England, it is the township assessor who determines the tax rate; the inspector who collects it; the town clerk who puts it in the public treasury and claims against it are heard in the common courts as they arise. Such a system of tax collection is slow and cumbersome; it interferes at every step with the working of a government with large financial demands. In general, one would hope that in areas of major importance, the government would select its own officials, accountable to it, with efficient ways of proceeding; but it will always be easy for centralized authority, organized as it is in America, to introduce, as necessary, means of operating that are more energetic and efficient.

The Republics of the New World will not perish, as has often been claimed, from lack of centralization; far from there being too little centralization, it can be said that the American governments have too much; I will prove that in due time. Every day the legislative assemblies are swallowing up more bits of governmental duties; they tend to take on everything, just as the [French] Convention did. Social power, thus centralized, is constantly changing hands, because it is subordinate to the authority of the people. It frequently happens that it lacks wisdom and foresight, because it is omnipotent. That is a threat to it. It may someday be destroyed as a result of its power, not its weakness.

Administrative decentralization produces several different results in America.

We have seen that the Americans have almost entirely isolated the administrative duties of government; in that they seem to me to have gone beyond the limits of sound reason; order, even in areas of secondary importance, is still in the national interest.

Lacking any administrative officials of its own in permanent positions throughout the country and who can be instilled with a common objective, the State rarely attempts to establish general rules of policing. The need for these rules is strikingly apparent. Europeans often remark on their absence. The appearance of disorder that prevails on the surface convinces them, at first, of a complete anarchy in the society; it is only by examining affairs in depth that they learn otherwise.

Some issues concern the whole state and yet cannot be addressed because there is no office in the national administration responsible for them. When these matters are left to towns and counties where they are assigned to elected and temporary officials they go nowhere, or result in nothing permanent.

Partisans of centralization in Europe maintain that governmental authority is better at running municipalities than they are at running themselves; that may be true, when the central authority is enlightened and the localities are without wise leaders, when government is active and localities stagnant, when the one is accustomed to governing and the other in the habit of obeying. We can even understand that as centralization grows, these two lines deepen, and the capacity of one and incapacity of the other become strikingly apparent.

When the people are enlightened, aware of their own interests and accustomed to reflecting on them, as people are in America, I would say that this does not happen.

I am persuaded, on the contrary, that in that case the collective strength of the citizens will always be more powerful in working for the good of society than the authority of government.

I admit that it is difficult to show with certainty how to awaken people from their sleep, how to instill in them a passion and wisdom that they lack; persuading men that they should participate in their own affairs is, I know, a difficult undertaking. It would often be less difficult to interest them in the details of court etiquette than in improving their shared dwelling.

But I also think that when the central administration claims to replace entirely the free participation of those most interested, it fools itself or is trying to fool you.

A central power, as enlightened or wise as one might think it, cannot alone encompass all the details of life of a great people. It cannot, because such a task exceeds human ability. When it wishes, by itself, to create and run so many different activities, it settles for a partial result, or it exhausts itself in futile efforts.

Part II

Up to this point I have been examining institutions, I have looked over written laws, I have described the actual shape of political society in the United States.

Above all the institutions and beyond the forms there is a sovereign power and that is the people who change or remove laws at will.

Now I must introduce the ways this lawmaking authority functions: its instincts, passions and the hidden impulses moving it forward, slowing it down, or directing its irresistible progress; the results of this omnipotence, and the future before it.

CHAPTER 5

Why It Is Accurate to Say That in the United States, the People Govern

In America, it is the people who make the laws and execute them; they make up the jury that punishes infractions against the law. Institutions are democratic not only on principle, but particularly in how they function; the people choose their representatives *directly*, and they choose them *every year*, in general holding them more fully accountable. It is truly the people who govern, and while the form of government is representative, it is obvious that the opinions, prejudices, interests, and even passions of the people encounter no permanent obstructions to their effective day-to-day running of society.

In the United States, and in every country where the people rule, the majority governs in the name of the people.

This majority is primarily composed of law-abiding citizens who, either by inclination or self-interest, sincerely desire the good of the

Chapter 5 appeared as Volume I, Part II, Chapter 1 in the original, complete text.

country. All around them, parties struggle endlessly to draw them to their side and gain the majority's support.

CHAPTER 6

The Real Advantages Derived by American Society from Democratic Government

[...]

PUBLIC SPIRIT IN THE UNITED STATES

In general, the love of country springs from unself-conscious, selfless, and indescribable sentiments that bind the heart of a man to the place of his birth. This instinctive love is mingled with a fondness for old ways, with respect for elders and nostalgia for the past; those who feel it cherish their homeland as they do their paternal home. They love the peace they have known there; they cling to the reassuring habits they formed there; they cling to memories and even take some pleasure in submitting to life there. When this love of homeland is heightened by religious zeal, as often happens, it can do amazing things. It becomes itself a sort of religion; it is irrational, it believes, feels, acts. One meets people who have managed to see the homeland personified in the monarch. They have projected on him some of their feelings of patriotism; they are filled with pride in his triumphs and are proud of his power. There was a time, under the old regime, when the French people felt a sort of joy submitting irrevocably to the arbitrary power of the monarch, stating proudly: "We live under the most powerful king in the world."

Like all unthinking passions, this love of country promotes efforts of fleeting greatness more than sustained efforts. After rescuing the state in times of crisis, it often leaves it to perish in times of peace.

When people remain simple in their morals and their faith is strong, when society rests peacefully on the old order whose legitimacy is uncontested, we see this instinctive love of country flourish.

Chapter 6 appeared as Volume I, Part II, Chapter 6 in the original, complete text.

There is yet another, more rational form than this; it is perhaps less generous and less ardent, but it is more fruitful and enduring; this form is born of knowledge; it grows with the aid of laws, it increases with the exercise of rights and ends, in some way, by joining individual self-interest. A man understands the personal benefit of the country's good; he knows that the law allows him to be part of creating this benefit, and he participates in the prosperity of his country, first as something that is good for him, and then as something that belongs to him.

But sometimes, in the life of a people, the time comes when the old customs have altered, traditions have broken down, beliefs are shaken, the power of memory grown faint, and when the light of reason is still insufficient, political rights are uncertain or limited. Then men view the fatherland only dimly and without confidence; they no longer recognize their country in the soil, which they view as only lifeless dirt, nor in the customs of their elders, which they are taught to consider a burden; nor in religion which they have begun to doubt; nor in laws that are not of their own making, nor in legislators whom they fear and scorn. They do not recognize the familiar anywhere, and withdraw into narrow and irrational selfishness. Such men take refuge in prejudice and fail to recognize the power of reason; they have neither the instinctive patriotism of monarchy, nor the deliberate patriotism of the republic; they are stuck between the two, amidst confusion and misery.

What can be done in such a situation? Regress. However, nations can no more return to youthful feelings than a man can to the innocent pleasures of childhood; they may miss them, but they cannot rekindle them. Therefore, one must move forward and hasten to make people see that self-interest is in the national interest, for selfless love of country has departed, never to return.

Certainly I am far from claiming that all men must be granted full political rights immediately in order to achieve this; but I am saying that the most powerful means of involving men in the future of their country, and perhaps the only one left to us, is for them to participate in government. In our day, civic-mindedness seems to me inseparable from the exercise of political rights; I believe that in the future we will find that the number of citizens rises or falls in direct proportion to the spread of these rights.

How is it that in the United States, whose inhabitants arrived so recently to the land they now occupy, bringing with them neither customs nor memories; where they meet for the first time people they do not recognize; where, in a word, there can hardly exist a sense of homeland: how is it that everyone is involved in the running of his town, his county, and his entire country, as if they were his own? The answer is that everyone, in his own way, takes an active part in governing society.

In the United States, a man of the people understands the impact that the general prosperity has on his own happiness, an idea so simple and yet so little known by people. Moreover, he is accustomed to considering prosperity as his own responsibility. He sees in the public good his own benefit and he works for the good of the State, not only from duty or pride, but also from what I would boldly call greed.

We do not need to study American institutions and history to see the truth of what I have said, it is clear from the manners and customs. The American who is involved in everything that goes on in that country believes himself responsible for defending it against all criticism; to criticize the country is to criticize him personally; in his national pride he has resorted to all manner of foolishness and become childishly conceited.

There is nothing as annoying in daily life as this irritable patriotism among Americans. The visitor finds many things he would gladly praise about their country; but sometimes he would like to be allowed to point out faults, and that is what is absolutely forbidden.

America is thus a free country where, in order to avoid offending anyone, the visitor may not speak freely about individuals or the State, about the governed or the governors, or about public or private enterprise; about nothing that one observes except perhaps the climate and the soil; and one meets Americans ready to defend them one and all, as if they had all united to create them.

Today we must make up our minds and dare to choose between the patriotism of the masses and government of the few, for it is impossible to join both the strength and social activism of the first with the assurance of order that the latter can sometimes offer. [. . .]

ACTIVITY PREVAILING IN ALL PARTS OF THE BODY POLITIC IN THE UNITED STATES AND ITS INFLUENCE ON SOCIETY

Traveling from a free country into one that is not free, one is struck by an extraordinary sight: in the former, everything is active and in flux; in the second, everything seems calm and static. In the first, everything is improving and progressing; whereas in the other, after attaining greatness, the society aspires only to sit back and enjoy it. The country in which so much energy is spent on being happy is usually richer and more prosperous than the one that appears content. And in examining them together, it is hard to understand how people in the first seem to identify a new need every day, while in the second seem conscious of so few.

While this is true in free countries that have retained the monarchical form and in those where aristocracy rules, it is even more so in democratic republics. There, it is not only some people who are involved in improving the state of society, rather everyone who feels some responsibility for it. It is not simply a matter of providing for the needs and comforts of one class, but of all classes simultaneously.

As soon as you set foot on American soil, you find yourself in the middle of a tumult; a confusing clamor is heard on all sides, a thousand voices heard at once, each one expressing some social need. Around you, everything is in motion; here, the people of one neighborhood have gathered to decide whether to build a church; there, they are trying to choose a representative; further on, county representatives are rushing to town in order to debate some local improvements; elsewhere, village farmers have left their fields to discuss plans for a new road or school. Some citizens gather for the sole purpose of declaring that they disapprove of some government process, while others meet to proclaim that those in office are fathers of the country. There are others still who, seeing drunkenness as the source of all the ills of the state, solemnly meet to dedicate themselves to temperance.

The great political movement that constantly stirs up American legislatures, all that is seen from outside, is just one episode and a kind of extension of this universal movement, one which begins in the lowest ranks of the people and moves closer and closer to every class of citizens. It would be impossible for anyone to work harder to be happy.

It is difficult to say what place interest in public policy has in the life of an individual in the United States. To be involved in governing and talking about it is of utmost importance and could be called an American's sole recreation. This is apparent in the smallest details of his life; women themselves often attend public assemblies, taking a break from their housework to listen to political speeches. For them, the clubs take the place of theaters. An American does not converse, he argues; he does not engage in discourse, he holds forth at length. He always speaks as if to an assembly, and if he should happen to grow heated, he will address his listener as "Gentlemen."

In some countries, the people accept only with a sort of repugnance the political rights accorded to them by law; to them it would seem that time spent on the common good was time stolen, and they prefer to selfishly seal themselves off on four sides behind trenches and hedges.

By contrast, if an American were forced to concern himself with his personal business alone, he would lose half his life; he would feel an immense void in his days and he would grow incredibly depressed.

I am convinced that if despotism were ever to be established in America, it would find it more difficult to defeat these habits engendered by liberty than to overcome the love of liberty itself.

This constant restlessness that democratic government has introduced into politics permeates civil society as well. It may be that, on the whole, this is the greatest advantage of democratic government, and I appreciate much more what it allows to happen than what it does itself.

There is no question but that the people often manage their public affairs very badly; however, people who are involved in the political process cannot help broadening their perspectives and expanding their minds. The man of the people who is called upon to govern society develops considerable self-esteem. When he acquires power, people with very enlightened minds are available to assist him. People constantly seek his support, and he learns from a thousand different efforts to trick him. In politics, he participates in business he never even thought of, that give him a general taste for business. Every day he is shown new ways to improve public property; and a desire is born in him to improve his own private property. He is neither more virtuous nor happier, perhaps, but more informed and more active than his predecessors. I strongly believe that democratic institutions, combined with the physical nature of the country, are an indirect reason, and not the direct reason as many people would say, for the prodigious industrial expansion that everyone notices in the United States. It is not the laws that have produced this, but the people who learned to achieve it by making laws.

When enemies of democracy claim that a single person is better at handling his responsibilities than government by many, I think they are right. Government by one person, assuming equal intelligence on both sides, can provide greater continuity to affairs of state than does the multitude; it can demonstrate greater perseverance, a greater sense of the whole, a greater attention to detail, and be more discerning in judgment of people. Those who deny this have never seen a democratic republic, or have examined only a very few examples. For it is true that even when local government and the attitudes of the people enable democracy to work, it does not bring regular administrative oversight and managerial practices to governing. Free democracy does not execute all of its tasks with the same expertise as intelligent despotism; often it moves on before realizing success or risking failure; but in the long run the former is more productive than the latter; it performs each task less well, but it accomplishes more. Under its rule, the most important thing is not what public administration actually does, it is what happens without and outside it. Democracy does not give people the most efficient government, but it does what the most efficient government is often incapable of doing; it spreads throughout the social order a restless activity, a potent strength, an energy that never exists without it and that, as long as conditions are favorable, can create wonders. That is where democracy's real advantages lie.

In this century, when the fate of the Christian world seems uncertain, some hasten to attack democracy as a powerful enemy, as it grows ever stronger; others already worship it as some new god emerging from the chaos; however, neither side really understands the object of its dread or attraction; they do battle in the shadows and attack randomly.

What do you want from society and its government? That must be made clear.

Do you wish to elevate the human spirit, inspire a generous outlook on the things of this world? Do you wish to instill in men a scorn for material things? Do you want to inspire deep beliefs and cultivate great devotion?

Is it important to you to improve morals, elevate manners, and cultivate the arts? Do you desire poetry, acclaim, and glory?

Are you attempting to organize society to have a powerful influence on others: do you expect it to attempt great things, and, whatever the result of these efforts, to leave a lasting impression on history?

If you believe that is the primary goal of man in society, then do not support democratic government; it will definitely not lead you there.

But if it seems to you beneficial to divert man's moral and intellectual energy to the material needs of life, and to use them to create prosperity; if you think reason is of more use to man than genius; if your objective is not to create heroic virtues but habits of moderation; if you prefer some vices to crime and would give up acts of greatness for fewer heinous crimes; if you would settle for living in a prosperous society rather than in one of striking brilliance; if, finally, the main purpose of government for you is not to build the strongest or most glorious nation possible, but to provide the greatest good and eliminate the most suffering for everyone, then establish equality of conditions and democratic government.

If there is not time to make a choice, and if a power beyond human control is already sweeping you forward, regardless of your preferences, toward either one of these governments, then at least try to derive the greatest good from it; and knowing both its best and worst instincts, strive to reinforce the former and limit the latter.

CHAPTER 7

The Omnipotence of the Majority in the United States and Its Consequences

The absolute sovereignty of the majority is the essence of democratic government; in a democracy, nothing outside the majority is capable of mounting resistance to it.

Most American constitutions have, in fact, contrived to expand the natural strength of the majority.

Among all the branches of power, legislatures respond most readily to the will of the majority. Americans prefer to elect their representatives directly and for very short terms as a means of requiring their obedience to constituents, to their general points of view as well as to their momentary passions.

Members of both houses are drawn from the same classes and appointed in the same way; consequently, legislative action is nearly as swift and no less potent than would be that of a single assembly.

Thus constituted, the legislatures have acquired almost all powers of government.

Even as the law has strengthened powers that were by nature very strong, it has further weakened those that were naturally weak. It granted the representatives of the executive branch neither stability nor independence; and in subordinating them completely to the

Chapter 7 appeared as Volume I, Part II, Chapter 7 in the original, complete text.

caprices of the legislature, it has deprived them of even the slight influence they would naturally have in a democratic government.

In several states, the law leaves the election of the judiciary to the will of the majority, and in all states the judiciary is dependent on the legislative branch that has the right to set the annual salary of judges.

Practice has even surpassed law.

A custom is spreading more and more in the United States that will ultimately render the guarantees of representative government useless; it very often happens that when voters elect a deputy they prescribe a plan of action that imposes a certain number of absolute obligations, which he cannot shirk. In tumultuous times it is as if the majority itself were deliberating in the public forum.

Several specific circumstances in America tend to make the power of the majority not only predominant, but also irresistible.

The moral superiority of the majority is based in part on the idea that there is more wisdom and talent in an assembly of men than in a single individual, that the number of legislators matters more than the choice. That is the theory of equality as applied to intelligence. This doctrine is an affront to human pride in its last refuge; and the minority acknowledges it reluctantly and takes a long time becoming accustomed to it. As with all powers, and perhaps more than any other, the power of the majority must endure to appear legitimate. When it is newly established, obedience must be forced; only after living under its laws for a long time do men come to respect it.

The right of an enlightened majority to govern society was a concept brought to American soil by the earliest inhabitants. This idea, which in itself would suffice to create a free people, has today become part of American mores and can be found in every detail of daily life.

Under the old regime, French people believed the king was infallible, and when he happened to do wrong, they blamed his advisers. This made obedience amazingly simple. One could complain about a law without ceasing to love and respect the ruler. Americans have that same view of the majority.

The moral supremacy of the majority is still based on the principle that the interests of the greatest number must be preferred to those of the few. Everyone knows of course that the respect expressed for the right of the majority naturally grows or shrinks according to circumstances. When a nation is divided by irreconcilable differences, the privilege of the majority is often out of favor, because submitting to it becomes too difficult.

If there had been a class of citizens in America that the legislature wanted to reduce in status to the level of the masses and it attempted to strip those citizens of centuries old, exclusive advantages, it is likely that the minority would not have submitted readily to its laws.

However, because the United States is populated by men equal to each other, there is as yet no natural and permanent disagreement among the diverse interests of the inhabitants.

There is a level of society in which the members of a minority cannot hope to gain the support of the majority, because to do so would be to abandon the very object of their conflict with the majority. Aristocracy, for example, cannot become a majority and still preserve its exclusive privileges, and it cannot surrender its privileges without ceasing to be an aristocracy.

In the United States, political questions cannot present themselves in such a broad and absolute manner, and all parties are willing to recognize the rights of the majority because all hope one day to benefit from it.

Thus, the majority's actual power in the United States is enormous and almost equal to the power of public opinion; once the majority has formed its opinion on any question, nothing can stop it or even block it long enough to allow time for the arguments of those who are crushed in the process to be heard.

The consequences of this state of affairs are deeply troubling and dangerous for the future.

THE OMNIPOTENCE OF THE MAJORITY INCREASES THE ADMINISTRATIVE AND LEGISLATIVE INSTABILITY NATURAL TO A DEMOCRACY

I have already written about the evils inherent in democratic government; all of these increase in proportion to the power of the majority.

To begin with the most obvious one of all:

Legislative instability is an inherent weakness of democratic government because it is in the nature of democracies to bring inexperienced people to power. This weakness is more or less important depending on the power and means given to the legislators.

In America, the authority that makes laws has supreme power. It can respond quickly and definitively to every desire, and every year it receives new representatives. This is, in short, the very combination that most encourages democratic instability and that allows democratic government to vacillate on issues of importance.

Consequently, of all countries today, American laws are the least enduring. Almost every American constitution has been amended in the last thirty years. There is no American state that has not, during this period, modified its legal principles.

As for the laws themselves, one glance at the records of the various states is enough to convince us that legislative activity never slows in America. Not because American democracy is inherently less stable than another, but because in lawmaking it has been enabled to follow its naturally fluctuating inclinations.

The supremacy of the majority and the speed and manner in which it executes its will in the United States not only leads to instability of laws but also has the same effect on the execution of laws and on acts of public administration.

Because it is necessary to cater only to the majority, the competition is fierce for the projects it undertakes, but as soon as it loses interest, all efforts cease; whereas in the free States of Europe, in which the administrative authority is independent and secure, the will of the legislature continues to be carried out even after it turns to other issues.

In America, much greater zeal and energy is spent on some improvements than on others.

In Europe, the social pressure on these same issues is infinitely smaller, but more continuous.

A few years ago, some religious leaders called for an improvement in conditions inside prisons. The public was moved by their appeals, and the rehabilitation of criminals became a popular issue.

New prisons were built. For the first time, the idea of *reforming* the guilty as well as punishing them penetrated the prisons. But the positive revolution which the public so warmly embraced and which was made irresistible by the simultaneous efforts of citizens, could not be achieved in a day.

Alongside the new penitentiaries whose development was hastened by the will of the majority, the old prisons remained and continued to contain a great number of offenders. The latter seemed to become increasingly unhealthy and corrupting as the new ones became more healthy and committed to reform. This dual result is understandable: the majority, preoccupied with the idea of founding the new order, had forgotten about the existing one. And so everyone looked away from the problems that no longer interested the masters; surveillance ceased. First, the salutary bonds of discipline were stretched and soon broken entirely. Next to the prison, a lasting monument to the gentleness and enlightenment of our age, there are dungeons that recall the barbarity of the Middle Ages.

THE TYRANNY OF THE MAJORITY

I consider detestable and blasphemous the maxim that in matters of government the majority of a people has a right to do whatever it wishes, and yet I place the origin of all powers in the will of the majority. Am I contradicting myself?

One universal law has been made, or at least adopted, not only by the majority in one country or another, but by a majority of all men. That law is justice.

Justice thus defines the boundary of the right of any country.

A nation is like a jury responsible for representing the entire society and for applying justice, which is its law. Should the jury representing society have greater authority than the very society whose law it applies?

When I refuse to obey an unjust law, therefore, I am not denying the right of the majority to rule; I am simply appealing to the sovereignty of the human race from the sovereignty of the people.

There are those who are not afraid to say that a people, in things that concern only themselves, are incapable of exceeding entirely the limits of justice and reason and that there is therefore no need to fear giving all power to the majority that represents them. But that is the language of slavery.

What is a majority, taken collectively, if not an individual with opinions, and most often interests, contrary to another individual we call the minority? If you agree that an all-powerful individual is capable of abusing his power to harm his opponents, why not admit that the same is true for the majority? Do men, when they form groups, change character? Do they become more patient with obstacles when they become more powerful? For my part, I don't think so; and the power to do whatever one likes, which I would not give to any one of my fellow men, I will never grant to the many.

It is not because I believe that, to guard liberty, we can combine several principles in the same government in real opposition to each other.

A so-called mixed government has always seemed to me an illusion. There is, to be honest, no mixed government (in the normal sense of this word), because in every society some guiding principle is found that dominates all the others.

In the eighteenth century, England was often cited as an example of one such government, remaining an essentially aristocratic state even while embracing major elements of democracy; laws and mores there were so established that the aristocracy would always, in the long run, predominate and rule over public affairs.

The error lay in always seeing the interests of the mighty as struggling against those of the people, and thinking only about the contest without paying attention to the result of this struggle, which was the important thing. When a society reaches the point of having a truly mixed government, one that is equally divided between conflicting principles, there will be a revolution or the society will collapse.

I believe, therefore, that it is always necessary for a national power to be established somewhere above the others, but I also believe that liberty is imperiled when that power finds no obstacle in its path capable of slowing its progress and giving it time to moderate itself.

Omnipotence in itself seems to me a bad and dangerous thing. Exercising it seems to me beyond the power of any man, whoever he is, and I think only God can safely be called all-powerful, because his justice and wisdom are always equal to his power. There is no authority on earth so respectable in itself, or endowed with such a sacred right, that I would allow it to act without control and rule unimpeded. Whenever I see any sovereign given supreme right and power, whether that authority is called the people or the king, democracy or aristocracy, whether in a monarchy or a republic, I say: that is where the seed of tyranny lies, and I seek to live under a different law.

What I most fault democratic government for, as it is organized in the United States, is not its weakness, as many in Europe claim, but the opposite, its irresistible power. And what I detest most in America is not the extreme liberty that prevails there, but the few protections against tyranny.

When a man or a party suffers injustice in the United States, to whom will he turn? to public opinion? but that is shaped by the majority; to the legislative body? that represents the majority and obeys it blindly; to the executive branch? that is named by the majority and serves it passively; to the police? a police force is simply the majority given arms; to a jury? a jury is the majority given the right to pronounce sentence; even judges, in several states, are elected by the majority. However unfair or unreasonable a measure that harms you may be, you must submit to it.

Imagine, however, a legislative body composed in such a way that it represents the majority without necessarily being a slave to its will; an executive power with the authority appropriate to it, and a judicial power independent of the others: that would be a democratic government, but there would no longer be any possibility of tyranny.

I am not saying that at present acts of tyranny occur frequently in America, but I am saying that there is no guarantee against it there, and that the basis for goodness in government is not found in laws but in mores and circumstances.

THE ARBITRARY POWER OF AMERICAN PUBLIC OFFICIALS AS A CONSEQUENCE OF THE ALL-POWERFUL MAJORITY

It is important to distinguish between arbitrary power and tyranny. Tyranny can work through the law itself, at which point it is not at all arbitrary; the arbitrary can work on behalf of the governed and then is not tyrannical.

Tyranny often resorts to arbitrary power, but it can do without it when necessary.

In the United States, the omnipotence of the majority encourages arbitrary judicial action while simultaneously encouraging legal legislative despotism. The majority, having absolute authority for making and executing the law, and having equal authority over both governors and governed, views public officials as passive agents and willingly grants them the responsibility for serving its purposes. Consequently, it does not involve itself in advance in the details of their duties and hardly goes to the trouble of defining their rights. It treats them as a master would his servants if they were constantly in view so that he could direct or correct their activities on the spot.

In general, the law gives American officials much more freedom than ours within their defined spheres. It even happens sometimes that the majority allows them to step outside the limits. Protected by majority opinion and strengthened by its support, they dare to do something even Europeans, accustomed to the sight of arbitrary action, find shocking. In the heart of liberty some habits are taking root that may one day be dangerous to freedom.

THE POWER EXERCISED BY THE MAJORITY OVER THOUGHT IN AMERICA

Once we begin to examine the role of public opinion in America it becomes quite apparent that the power of the majority there surpasses any power we know in Europe.

Public opinion is an invisible power and one that is almost impossible to grasp; it has a role in every tyranny. Today, even the most absolute rulers of Europe are unable to stop certain ideas, hostile to their authority, from circulating secretly in their States and even in their own courts. It is not the same in America: people will talk as long as the majority view is in question; but its word, once expressed, is irrevocable, and everyone falls quiet, with friends and enemies alike seeming to jump on board. The reason for this is simple: there is no power so absolute that it can hold in one hand all social forces and overcome all resistance except a majority armed with the right both to make and to execute the law.

Moreover, a king has only physical power, allowing him to govern men's actions but not their will; the majority, however, is invested with both physical and moral authority, which acts on the will as well as on behavior; it prevents the act as well as the desire to act.

I know of no country in which there exists, generally speaking, less independence of mind and real freedom of debate than America.

There is no religious or political theory that people cannot preach freely in the constitutional states of Europe and that does not spread into the others; for there is no country in Europe so submissive to a single authority that a person wishing to speak the truth there cannot find some support capable of protecting him from retaliation for his independence. If he has the misfortune to live under an absolute ruler, he often has the people on his side; if he lives in a free country, he might, if necessary, find shelter in the power of the ruler. The aristocratic element of society will support him in democratic countries, and democracy will support him in others. But at the heart of a democracy organized like that in the United States, one will find only one power, a single source of power and success, and nothing outside it.

In America, the majority draws a formidable circle around thought. Within its limits, the writer is free; but woe to anyone who dares to go beyond it. Not because he fears an inquisition but because he will be the object of all kinds of outrage and of daily attacks. He will have no political future: he has offended the only power that could offer one. He will be denied everything, even glory. He may have thought, before his opinions were published, that he had supporters; he will feel that he hasn't a single one left, once he has revealed himself to all; for those who disagree will be vocal, and those who agree with him, lacking his courage, remain quiet and distant. He yields, buckling under the effort every day, and retreats into silence, as if remorseful for having spoken the truth.

Chains and hangmen, these were the blunt instruments that tyranny once wielded; today civilization has surpassed even despotism itself, which was once thought to have gone as far as it could.

Monarchs had, so to speak, made violence physical; the democratic republics of our day have made violence as intellectual as the human will that they wish to constrain. Under the absolute government of a single ruler, despotism attacked the spirit by attacking the body; and the spirit, escaping the blows, rose gloriously above them; but in the democratic republics, this is not how tyranny proceeds; it leaves the body alone and goes straight for the spirit. The master no longer says: You will think as I do, or you will die; he says: You are free not to think at all as I do; your life, your property, everything is yours; but from this day on you are a stranger among us. You will retain the privileges of citizenship, but they will be useless to you; for if you seek the approval of your fellow citizens, it will be denied, and if you ask only their respect, they will still find some pretense for refusing you. You will remain among men, but you will lose your right to humanity. When you approach your fellow men, they will shun you as someone tainted; and those who believe in your innocence, they too will desert you, for they will be shunned in turn. Go in peace, I will let you live, but I give you a life worse than death.

Absolute monarchs disgraced despotism; let us take care that democratic republics not restore it, and, while making it more oppressive for the few, strip it of its odious and malicious character in the eyes of the majority.

In the proudest nations of the Old World, works were published that were intended to be a faithful picture of the vices and absurdities of contemporary society; La Bruyère lived in the court of Louis XIV when he wrote his chapter on the mighty, and Molière criticized the court in his plays written to be performed for courtiers. But the power that dominates in the United States will not be mocked. The lightest rebuke wounds, the slightest needling of truth enrages. One must praise everything from linguistic forms to solid virtues. No writer, however distinguished, escapes this obligation to heap praise upon his fellow citizens. Thus the majority enjoys perpetual adoration; only foreigners or personal experience can bring certain truths to American ears.

If America has not yet produced any great writers, we don't have to look far to find the reasons: literary genius cannot exist without freedom of thought, and there is no freedom of thought in America.

The inquisition in Spain was never able to prevent the circulation of books that opposed the religion of most people. The sovereignty of the majority has done better in the United States; it has removed any thought of publishing such a book. There are disbelievers in America, but disbelief has no voice there.

There are some governments that struggle to protect morals by condemning the authors of licentious books. In the United States, no one is condemned for books of that type; but no one is tempted to write them. This is not because all citizens have pure morals, but the morals of the majority are conventional.

Here, the use of power is undoubtedly for the good; I was speaking about the power itself. This irresistible power is a constant reality, and its good use is only an accident.

THE EFFECT OF THE TYRANNY OF THE MAJORITY ON THE AMERICAN CHARACTER AND THE COURTIER SPIRIT IN THE UNITED STATES

The influence of what I have just written is only faintly felt in political society; but one notices already some troubling effects on the national character of Americans. I think the ever-growing despotism of the majority in the United States is the reason for the small number of great men who appear today on the political scene.

When the American Revolution broke out, there were many such men; public opinion directed the popular will but did not tyrannize it. The famous men of that period, identifying freely with the movement of ideas, had the stature that befitted them: they cast glory on the nation rather than taking from it.

In absolute governments, the important men who surround the throne flatter the passions of the master and voluntarily bow to his caprices. But most people in the country are not part of this servitude; they usually obey out of weakness, habit, or ignorance; sometimes out of love for the monarchy or the king. We have seen some who take a kind of pleasure and pride in sacrificing their will to that of the king, thus putting independence of mind at the center of their obedience. Among those people, we find less degradation than suffering. There is moreover a great difference between doing what one doesn't approve and pretending to approve what one does; one is an act of weakness, but the other attitude is befitting only of a valet.

In free countries, where each person is more or less called upon to offer his opinion on the affairs of state, and in democratic republics, where public life is constantly joining with private life, where the sovereign is approachable by all, and to be heard one need only speak up, we meet many more people who are willing to gamble on the ruler's weakness and live off of his passions than are found in absolute monarchies. It is not that men there are naturally worse than elsewhere, but the temptation is greater and available to more people at the same time. It leads to a much more general decline in character.

Democratic republics have put this sort of valet mentality within reach of the masses and allowed it to penetrate all classes simultaneously. That is one of its principal failings.

It is especially true in democratic states organized on the American model, in which the majority possesses such absolute and irresistible control that one must in some way renounce his rights of citizenship and even his manhood if he decides to leave the prescribed path.

Among the great multitude rushing into politics in the United States, I have seen very few who demonstrate the virile candor, the manly independence of thought, that often distinguished the Americans of an earlier time and which, wherever it is found, is the outstanding characteristic of people of great character. At first glance, one might say that in America all minds have been formed alike, so exactly do they conform to the same paths. It is true, foreigners may sometimes meet Americans who depart from the usual clichés; some have come to hate the evils of their laws, the inconsistency of democracy, and its lack of enlightened thinkers; often they go so far as to remark on the failings that have altered the national character, and they point out the ways one might correct these; but you are the only one listening; and you, to whom they confide their inner thoughts, are just a foreigner, and you are going to leave. They gladly reveal truths that are useless for you, and then, once back in public, it's a different story.

If these lines ever appear in America, I know two things: first, that all readers will raise their voices to condemn me; and second, that there will be many who, in their hearts, will acquit me.

I have heard people speak of the fatherland in the United States. I have encountered true patriotism among the people; I have often sought it in vain among the leaders. This is easily understood by analogy: despotism corrupts the one who submits to it more than the one who imposes it. In absolute monarchies, the king is often highly virtuous; it is the courtiers who are always base.

It is true that in America courtiers never call their leaders Sire or Majesty, and consider that an important distinction; but they speak constantly about the natural wisdom of their ruler; they never ask which of the leader's virtues is most to be admired; for they insist that he possesses all virtues, without having to acquire them, and in a way without even wanting them; they do not offer him their wives and daughters to take as mistresses; but, by sacrificing their own opinions, they prostitute themselves.

In America, moralists and philosophers are not required to wrap their views in the veils of allegory; but, before risking a troubling truth, they say: we know that we are speaking to a people so far above human weakness that they will always remain masters of themselves. We would never speak like this if we were not addressing men whose goodness and enlightenment render them alone worthy of remaining free.

Could the flatterers at the court of Louis XIV have done better than this?

For my part, I believe that in every government, no matter what kind, servility will be a partner of strength and flattery of power. I know of only one way to stop men from degrading themselves: that is to give no one the omnipotence, the sovereign power, to debase them.

THE GREATEST THREAT TO THE AMERICAN REPUBLICS IS THE OMNIPOTENCE OF THE MAJORITY

Governments ordinarily perish from weakness or from tyranny. In the first case, they lose power; in the second, it is taken from them.

Many people, watching democratic states collapse in anarchy, have thought that the government in those states was naturally weak and powerless. The truth is that, once war breaks out between factions, government loses effectiveness over society. However, I do not think that by its nature democratic power lacks strength and resources; I believe, on the contrary, that it is almost always the abuse of its powers and the misuse of its resources that cause it to perish. Anarchy is almost always born of tyranny or incompetence, not of weakness.

It is important not to confuse stability with might, size, and durability. In democratic republics, the power that governs society is not stable, for it often changes hands and objectives. But, wherever it goes, its strength is almost irresistible.

The government of the American republics seems as centralized and even more energetic than that of the absolute monarchies of Europe. I do not believe that they will fail through weakness.

If Americans ever lose their freedom, it will be the fault of the omnipotent majority that will have driven the minority to despair and forced them to take up arms. We will then see anarchy, the consequence of despotism.

CHAPTER 8

What Tempers the Tyranny of the Majority

[. . .]

THE JURY IN THE UNITED STATES CONSIDERED AS A POLITICAL INSTITUTION

[. . .]

To see the role of the jury as a strictly judicial institution is to take a very narrow view of the matter; it has a tremendous influence on the outcome of the trial, and even greater on the fate of society itself. A jury is above all a political institution. This is the point of view from which it must be judged.

By "jury" I mean a group of citizens chosen at random and momentarily invested with the right to judge.

Using a jury to punish criminal activity seems to me to introduce a particularly republican element into government. Let me explain:

A jury system may be aristocratic or democratic depending upon the class from which jurors are drawn; however, it will always have a republican element in that it puts the actual management of society

---

Chapter 8 appeared as Volume I, Part II, Chapter 8 in the original, complete text.

in the hands of the governed, or some of them, and not in the hands of the governors. [. . .]

I am so convinced that the jury is above all a political institution that I view it as such when it applies to civil matters as well.

Laws that are not backed up by mores are always somewhat precarious; mores provide a nation its only solid and enduring strength.

When the jury is reserved for criminal affairs, people see it working only from afar and in special cases; they grow accustomed to ignoring it in their daily lives, and consider it as simply one means, although not the only means, of obtaining justice.

When, on the contrary, the work of a jury reaches into civil affairs, its application can be seen everywhere and concerns everyone; all participate in it; it reaches into the habits of daily life; its procedures shape the human mind and virtually blend into the definition of justice.

Consequently, when the jury system is restricted to criminal affairs, it is always at risk; once juries are introduced into civil affairs, they stand up to the passing of time and the assaults of men. If the jury system had been as easily removed from English mores as it was from the law, it would have died out completely under the Tudors. It was actually civil juries that saved England's liberties.

No matter how it is applied, a jury will always have a great influence over national character; but its influence is infinitely greater when it moves into civil cases.

A jury, and especially a civil jury, teaches all citizens to think like judges, to acquire some of their ways of thinking, and these are the very ways of thinking that best prepare a people for freedom.

It spreads respect for the court's decisions and the concept of justice through every class. Take away these two concepts, and the love of independence is little more than a destructive passion.

It teaches men to exercise fairness. Every man knows, in judging his neighbor, that he will be judged in turn. That is true particularly of civil juries; almost no one fears involvement in criminal proceedings; but anyone may be subject to a lawsuit.

From juries, everyone learns to accept responsibility for his own actions; without that manly attitude, political virtue is impossible.

On a jury, everyone becomes a magistrate; all men are made aware of their obligations to society and the duty to participate in government. By obliging men to be responsible for more than their personal affairs, individual egoism, which corrodes society, is checked.

The jury is incredibly valuable in shaping the judgment and enhancing the natural abilities of a people. That, in my opinion, is its greatest asset. It must be viewed as a free education, a school that is always open, to which every juror can come to learn about his rights, where he has daily communication with the most educated and enlightened members of the higher classes, where he learns the laws in a practical way, and in a way he can understand, from lawyers, from the opinions of a judge and the passionate arguments of the parties involved. I think that the practical intelligence and sound political sense of Americans must be attributed to their long experience with juries in civil cases.

I do not know if the jury is useful to those involved in lawsuits, but I am certain that it is valuable to those who must judge them. I consider it to be one of a society's most effective means of educating its people.

All of the above applies to all nations; but what I have to say now is specific to Americans and in general to democratic societies.

I said earlier that in democracies, lawyers, including magistrates, form the only aristocratic body that can moderate popular movements. This aristocracy is invested with no material power; its conservative influence works only on the mind. The main sources of its power reside in the institution of civil juries.

In criminal trials, where society is pitted against an individual, the jury comes to see in the judge the passive instrument of social power, and to mistrust his point of view. Moreover, criminal trials involve simple facts that are grasped by common sense. In such matters, the judge and jury are equals.

This is not the case in civil trials; then the judge appears as an impartial arbiter between the passions of two parties. The jurors look upon him with confidence, and listen to him with respect; in these cases, his intelligence is superior to theirs. It is he who unravels for them the wearisome arguments and who leads them through the many complexities of the case. He helps them adhere to the facts and answers their questions on points of law. His influence over them is almost unlimited.

Must I still explain why arguments about the incompetence of jurors in civil matters do not sway me?

In civil suits, at least those in which matters of fact are not at issue, the jury is only superficially a judicial body.

The jury simply pronounces the judge's decision. It invests the decision with the authority of the society they represent, while the judge gives it the authority of reason and of law.

In England and America, judges exercise an influence over the outcome of criminal trials greater than any French judge has ever known. It is easy to see the reason for this difference: the authority of English and American magistrates is first established in civil cases; they may exercise it in other areas, but they do not acquire it there.

There are cases, and sometimes very important ones, where an American judge has the right to pronounce a decision alone. He may then find himself in the position of the French judge; but his moral authority is greater: memories of juries are never far from him, and his words have almost as much weight as when a jury speaks for society.

Moreover, his influence extends far beyond the limits of the courts: whether in his private relaxation or in the political fray, in the market-place or the legislature, an American judge is constantly surrounded by people who regard his intellect as superior to their own; and outside court proceedings his authority makes itself felt in the habits of thought and in the very soul of everyone who participated in the judgment.

Thus the jury, which might appear to diminish the power of the judiciary, is in fact the basis of its authority, and there is no country where judges are as powerful as in those in which the people share their privileges.

It is principally through the institution of civil juries that American judges can instill in every level of society what I call a legal mentality.

Therefore the jury, which is the most dynamic expression of the people's rule, is also the most efficient means of teaching them how to rule.

CHAPTER 9

The Principal Causes Tending to Preserve a Democratic Republic in the United States

[. . .]

INDIRECT INFLUENCE OF RELIGIOUS BELIEFS UPON POLITICAL SOCIETY IN THE UNITED STATES

[. . .]

I have shown above how religion acts directly on politics in the United States. I believe its indirect action is even more important and it is just

Chapter 9 appeared as Volume I, Part II, Chapter 9 in the original, complete text.

when it is silent about liberty that it best instructs Americans in the art of being free.

There is a countless multitude of sects in the United States. Every cult is different in its form of worship of the Creator, but all agree about men's responsibilities toward one another. Each sect worships God in its own way, but each one preaches the same morality in the name of God. For every individual, it is important that his religion be true, but that is not the case for society as a whole. Society has nothing to fear or to hope for from the next life; for it, what is most important is not that all citizens profess the true religion, but that they profess a religion. Moreover, all sects in the United States are united in Christianity, and Christian morality is the same everywhere.

One may well suppose that a certain number of Americans act more out of habit than conviction in their worship of God. In the United States the leader is Christian and hypocrisy must consequently be widespread; yet America is the place in the world where Christianity has retained the most real power over people's souls; and there is no better example of how useful and natural it is to man, for the country where it holds the most sway today is also the freest and most enlightened country.

I have already stated that in general American priests embrace civil liberty, even those who do not support religious liberty; however, they do not endorse any particular political system. They take care to stay out of politics and do not become involved in alliances of political parties. So we cannot say that in the United States religion influences laws or aspects of political opinion, but it does guide morality and, by regulating family life, it helps regulate the state.

I do not doubt for one second that the strict morality one observes in the United States is primarily the result of faith. Religion there is often powerless to help men resist the vast number of temptations fortune offers them. It is incapable of moderating the desire for wealth that everything arouses in him, but it reigns supreme in the souls of women, and women shape morality. Marriage is more respected in America than anywhere in the world, and the conception of conjugal happiness there is the highest and most honest.

In Europe, almost all of society's disorders arise in the home, and usually not far from the nuptial bed. That is where men develop their scorn for natural ties and the legitimate pleasures, as well as their taste for disorder, their restlessness of spirit, and their fickle desires. Shaken by the tumultuous passions that often trouble his home life, the European only reluctantly submits to the legislative powers of the state. When an American leaves the turmoil of politics and returns to the haven of the family, he finds an image of order and peace. There, all pleasures are simple and natural, and his joy innocent and calm. When he has attained happiness through a well-regulated life, he has no trouble conforming in both opinions and desires.

While the European seeks to escape domestic unhappiness by disturbing society, the American draws from his home life a love of order that he carries with him into affairs of state.

In the United States, religion does not only regulate morals, it shapes the mind as well.

Among Anglo-Americans, some profess Christianity because they believe in it, others because they are afraid to look as if they do not believe. Christianity prevails without obstacles, professed by all; as a result, as I have said elsewhere, everything in the moral sphere is certain and fixed, whereas the political world seems given over to discussion and experimentation. Thus the human spirit never confronts an unlimited field: no matter how bold, it finds from time to time that it must pause before insurmountable obstacles. The boldest ideas, before innovation, must submit to certain customs that slow and restrain them.

As a result, the imagination of the Americans, even at its most radical, proceeds hesitantly, with circumspection; it is self-conscious and its measures incomplete. This restraint is carried over into political life and quite singularly favors the tranquility of the people, as well as the survival of the institutions they have adopted. Nature and circumstances have made the inhabitants of the United States bold; that is apparent from the way they pursue wealth. If the minds of Americans were free of all impediments, one would quickly find the boldest innovators and the most implacable logicians in the world among them. But American revolutionaries must ostensibly profess a certain respect for Christian morality and fairness, which prevents the easy violation of laws that would restrict the execution of their plans; and if they were to rise above their own scruples, they would still feel restrained by those of their supporters. Up to this time, there has been no one in the United States who would dare to espouse the maxim that everything is permissible in the service of society; an impious maxim, seemingly invented in a century of freedom to give legitimacy to all future tyrants.

Thus, while the law allows the American people freedom to do anything, religion prevents them from imagining and forbids them from daring too much.

Religion, which never mixes directly in government in America, must be regarded as their primary political institution, for though it did not give them the taste for freedom, it has singularly facilitated the use of freedom.

Americans themselves consider their religious beliefs from this point of view. I do not know if all Americans have religious faith, for who can read the depths of a heart? But I am sure that they believe it necessary to maintaining republican institutions. This is not the opinion of a single class or of a party, but of the nation as a whole; it is found at all levels.

In the United States, when a politician attacks a sect, even those who belong to that sect may continue to support him, but if he attacks all sects, everyone abandons him and he stands alone.

When I was in America, a witness testified in the county court of Chester (in the State of New York) that he did not believe in the existence of God or in the immortality of the soul. The judge refused to allow his testimony under oath, since, he said, the witness had destroyed in advance the faith one might have in his word. Newspapers reported the fact without comment.

Americans have so completely combined Christianity and freedom in their minds that it is almost impossible for them to imagine one without the other. And for them this is not at all a matter of sterile beliefs inherited from the past, something that is not really alive but dormant deep in the soul.

I have seen Americans form associations to send priests to the new Western states, to found schools and churches there; they fear that religion might be lost in the middle of the wilderness, and the people raised there might not be as free as those from whom they sprang. I have met rich inhabitants of New England who abandoned the land of their birth in order to help establish, on the banks of the Missouri or on the prairies of Illinois, the foundations of Christianity and of freedom. In the United States, religious zeal is constantly fed by the fire of patriotism. It would be a mistake to think that such people are thinking only of the next life; eternity is only one of their concerns. When you question these missionaries about Christian civilization, you will be surprised to hear them speak as often about worldly goods, and to find politicians where you would expect to find only priests. "All American republics are united," they will say; "If the republics of the west were to fall into anarchy, or submit to the yoke of despotism, the republican institutions that flourish along the Atlantic coast would be threatened; it is thus in our interest to ensure that the new States are religious, so that they allow us to remain free."

These are the opinions of Americans; but their error is obvious; every day some pedant informs me that everything in America is fine except that very religious spirit I admire; and I am told that on the other side of the Ocean freedom and the happiness of the human race lack only [Baruch] Spinoza's belief in the eternity of the world and [Pierre] Cabanis's assertion that the brain secretes thought. To that I have no response, except to say that people who say such things have never been to America, and have never seen either a religious people or a free people. I await their return.

There are some in France who consider republican institutions as fleeting tools for their own self-serving benefit. They view the immense distance between their vices and their poverty from power and wealth and wish to fill in this abyss with ruins in an effort to fill it. Their position toward freedom is akin to that of paid soldiers toward medieval kings: they wore the king's colors while waging war for their own profit. However, the republic will last long enough to raise them from their current vices. I am not speaking to them, but to others, who see the Republic as a permanent and peaceful state, a vital goal toward which ideas and mores are every day leading modern society, and who sincerely wish to prepare men for freedom. When such people attack religious belief, they are following their passions and not their best interests. Despotism can do without faith, but not freedom. Religion is much more necessary to the republic they advocate than it is to the monarchy they attack, and more important to democratic republics than to all others. How is society expected to survive once political ties are dropped if moral ties are not strengthened, and what will become of a nation that rules itself if it is not subject to God? [. . .]

THE UNDERLYING CAUSES FOR THE STRENGTH OF RELIGION IN AMERICA

[. . .]

As long as religion is based exclusively upon feelings that offer relief from all suffering, it will appeal to the human heart. When combined with the bitter passions of this world, it is sometimes forced to defend allies that provide more tangible support than love; and it must reject as enemies some who love it still, and fight those with whom it is joined. Religion cannot share in the material strength of governments without taking upon itself some of the hatreds governments breed.

The survival of political powers that seem the most established is guaranteed only by the opinions of a generation, the interests of a century, or often the life of one man. One law can change even the most absolute and entrenched social condition, and with it everything changes.

Society's powers are all more or less fleeting, as are our years on earth; one succeeds another with rapidity, as do the various troubles of life; and there has never been a government that could depend upon some permanent disposition of the human heart, nor one based on some immortal standard.

So long as a religion derives its strength from the feelings, instincts, and passions that we have seen reproduced in every age throughout history, it shall withstand the force of time, or at least it will be defeated only by another religion. But when religion seeks support in worldly interests, it becomes almost as fragile as any power on earth. Alone, it may achieve immortality; once it is bound with ephemeral powers, it will share their fate, and often collapses along with the temporal passions that supported them.

In joining with different political powers, religion can achieve nothing but an onerous alliance. It does not need their support to survive and may perish in serving them.

This danger that I have warned against exists in every age, but it is not always so apparent.

There have been centuries when governments seemed immortal, and others when one would say that the existence of a country was more fragile than that of a man.

Some constitutions keep its citizens in a state of lethargic sleep, and others keep them in a feverish state of agitation.

When governments seem strong and laws stable, men are unaware of the danger to religion of uniting itself with power.

When governments are clearly weak and laws subject to change, we are struck by the threat, but then it is often too late to avoid it. It is important, then, to learn to see it from afar.

When a nation adopts a democratic social state and we see the republic as a model for society, it becomes increasingly dangerous to combine church and state; the time will come when power will change hands, when one political theory will succeed another, when men, laws, even constitutions will disappear or be different every day, and not just once but continually. Turmoil and instability are in the very nature of democratic republics, just as stagnation and somnolence shape the law of absolute monarchies.

If the Americans, who elect a head of State every four years, legislators every two years, and replace provincial administrators every year and who have left politics to novices; if they had not put religion beyond politics, what would it have to hold onto in the ebb and flow of public opinion? In the middle of partisan fighting, where would it find the respect it is due? What would happen to its permanency when everything around it was disappearing?

The American clergy were the first to recognize this reality, and they have responded to it. They saw that, if they wanted political power, they would have to renounce their religious influence, and they preferred to do without the support of authority to having to share its vicissitudes.

In America, religion is perhaps less powerful than it has been in some periods and for some peoples, but its influence is more lasting. Forced to be self-reliant, nothing threatens it; acting only within its own sphere, it operates freely and without restraint. [. . .]

THE RELEVANCE OF THE PRECEDING REMARKS FOR EUROPE

[. . .]

Should we not then think about the gradual development of democratic institutions and values, not as something better but as the only means left to us of remaining free; and without loving democratic government, would we not be inclined to adopt it as the best and most honest solution to the social evils of today?

It is difficult to make people participate in government; it is even more difficult to give them what they lack, the experience and desire necessary for governing well.

In a democracy, desires are constantly changing; its agents are uncultured; its laws imperfect, I know. But if it were true that very soon there would be no intermediary between the reign of democracy and the yoke of a single ruler, should we not lean toward the first rather than submit voluntarily to the second? And if full equality were ultimately to become necessary, would it not be better to be equals in freedom than under a despot?

Those who, after having read this book, believe that in writing it I meant to suggest that everyone in a socially democratic state imitate the laws and values of the Anglo-Americans will be quite mistaken;

they will have retained the form but lost the substance of my argument. My aim has been to show, in the American example, that laws and especially values might allow a democratic people to remain free. I am, otherwise, very far from believing that we should follow the example democracy in America has set, and imitate the means it has used to attain this goal; I cannot ignore the influence that geography and history have had on its political constitutions, and I would regard it as a great misfortune for the human race if liberty had always to look the same everywhere.

However, I think that if we do not manage to introduce slowly and ultimately establish democratic institutions among ourselves, and if we fail to give all citizens the ideas and desires that will help prepare them for liberty, and finally allow them to enjoy it, there will be freedom for no one, neither bourgeois nor noble, rich nor poor, but equal tyranny for all; and I predict that if we fail here to found the peaceable rule of the greatest number in time, we will sooner or later reach the point of *unlimited* rule by one man.

CHAPTER 10

A Few Remarks on Present and Probable Future Conditions of the Three Races Living within the United States

The primary task I set for myself is now completed; I have described as fully as possible the laws and mores of American democracy. However, if I were to go no further, I would risk leaving my readers dissatisfied.

Beyond its immense and full democracy, we encountered another aspect of America; the people inhabiting the New World should be observed from more than one point of view.

The subject of this work has often led me to speak of Indians and blacks, but I have never had time to pause long enough to show the position of the two races living in the midst of the democratic country

---

Chapter 10 appeared as Volume I, Part II, Chapter 10 in the original, complete text.

I wished to describe; I spoke of the spirit that guided and the laws that aided in the formation of the Anglo-American confederation; I could describe only briefly, and very incompletely, the dangers that threaten this confederation, and it seemed to me impossible to analyze in detail, beyond these laws and mores, what chance the confederation had of surviving. In speaking of the union of states, I did not risk conjecturing about the permanence of the republican models in the new world, and, while alluding frequently to the widespread commercial activity in the Union, I did not concern myself with the future of the Americans as a commercial people.

These issues, which touch upon my subject, were not addressed; they concern Americans but not democracy, and it was the democracy in particular that I wished to portray. So I chose to delay addressing these issues; now in closing, I must return to them.

The territory occupied or claimed by the United States today reaches from the Atlantic Ocean to the shores of the Pacific. To the east and west, its borders are those of the continent itself; it extends south to the tropics and north to the glaciers.

The people spread across this expanse are not, as in Europe, offspring of the same family. From the beginning there have been three distinct, and I might almost say hostile, races living on the land. Differences in education, laws, origins, and even physical appearance have created an almost insurmountable barrier between them; fortune has brought them together on the same land, but it has thrown them together without blending them, and each race has followed its own destiny.

Among these very diverse people the first to attract our notice and the most educated, most powerful, and most fortunate is the white man, the European, the man *par excellence*; the Negro and Indian are in an inferior position. These two races do not have birth, appearance, language, or customs in common, but only their suffering. They occupy an equally inferior position in the country they inhabit; both feel the effects of tyranny, and though they suffer in different ways, the source of their persecution is the same.

Considering what happens in the world, it seems that Europeans are to men of other races what human beings are to animals. They use them to serve themselves, and when they do not submit, destroy them.

With one stroke, oppression has deprived the descendants of Africans all the privileges of humanity! In the United States, the Negro has lost even the memory of his homeland; he never hears the language of his fathers spoken; he has forsaken their religion and forgotten their customs. Ceasing to belong to Africa, he nevertheless has acquired none of the benefits of Europe; he is caught between the two societies; he remains isolated between the two peoples; sold by one and repudiated by the other; nowhere in the world can he find even a partial reflection of his homeland except in the service of his master.

The Negro has no family; he cannot consider his wife as more than a temporary partner in pleasure, and when children are born, they are his equals.

Shall I call it a blessing, or one of God's angriest curses, this disposition of the soul that makes a man insensitive to the most extreme suffering, and often even leads to a kind of depraved attachment to the cause of his suffering?

Plunged into an abyss of evil, the Negro hardly feels his misfortune; enslaved through violence, the habit of servitude has given him the thoughts and ambitions of a slave; he admires his tyrants more than he hates them, and finds joy and pride in the servile imitation of those who oppress him.

His intelligence has sunk to the level of his soul.

The Negro becomes a slave at birth. I am mistaken: in fact he is frequently taken from his mother's womb and one could say that he is a slave even before his birth.

Needs and pleasures are equally useless to him; he has none. He understands with his first awareness of his own existence that he belongs to someone else, in whose interest it is to look after him; he perceives that it is not for him to control his own fate; it seems to him that thought itself, a gift of providence, is of no use to him, and he accepts quietly the pleasures of his low station.

When he becomes free, independence often seems a heavier chain than slavery; for throughout his existence, he has learned to submit to everything, except reason; and when reason becomes his only guide, he doesn't recognize its voice. A thousand needs beset him, and he lacks the knowledge and the necessary energy to resist them. Those needs are masters to be resisted, and he has learned only to submit and obey. He falls into a miserable state, one in which servitude protects and destroys.

Oppression has had no less influence on the Indian races, but it has had a different effect.

Before white people arrived in the New World, the inhabitants of North America lived peacefully in the woods. Exposed to the ordinary vicissitudes of the life of savages, they showed all the vices and virtues of uncivilized peoples. The Europeans have driven the Indian tribes deep into the wilderness, and condemned them to a life of rootless wandering, full of inexpressible suffering.

The savage nations are governed only by conviction and custom.

By weakening the sense of homeland among the Indians of North America, by disrupting their traditions and interrupting the links in tribal memory, by changing all their habits and increasing beyond measure their needs, European tyranny has left them more disorganized and uncivilized than they ever were. The moral and physical conditions of these people have grown worse as well, and they have become more barbaric with their worsening plight. Nevertheless, Europeans have not managed to change the nature of the Indians entirely, and with the power to destroy them, they have never had the power to police and control them.

The Negro has been moved to the outer limit of servitude; the Indian at the extreme limit of freedom. The impact of slavery on the former has hardly been more destructive than the influence of independence on the latter.

The Negro has lost ownership of his very self, and could control his own existence only by committing a sort of larceny.

The savage is left on his own as soon as he is capable of acting. He barely knows the authority of his own family; his will has never bowed before that of his peers; no one has taught him to distinguish between voluntary obedience and shameful subjugation, and he is ignorant of the very word *laws*. For him, freedom means avoiding all social bonds. He is content in this barbaric independence and would rather die than sacrifice any part of it. Civilization has little appeal for such a man.

A Negro tries in countless ways to join the society that rejects him; he bows to the wishes of his oppressors, adopts their opinions, and hopes, through imitation, to be taken for one of them. From birth he is told that his race is naturally inferior to that of the whites, and he almost believes it, feels ashamed. In every feature, he finds a trace of slavery, and if he were able, he would repudiate himself entirely.

The Indian, however, has an imagination filled with the noble claims of his birth. He lives and dies with these proud dreams. Far from wishing to adapt his customs to ours, he clings to his barbarism as a distinctive sign of his race and he rejects civilization perhaps less out of hatred for it than out of fear of becoming like Europeans.

The Indian prefers the resources of the wilderness to the perfection of our arts; to our tactics, untamed courage; to the depth of our planning, only the spontaneous instincts of his savage nature. In this unequal fight, he is the loser.

The Negro would like to be like the European, and he cannot. The Indian could manage to, up to a point, but is too proud to try. Servility has condemned one to slavery; pride has condemned the other to death.

I remember coming upon the cabin of a pioneer one day while traveling through the forests of Alabama. I did not wish to intrude in the home of the American, but wanted to rest a few moments beside a spring not far from there in the woods. While I was there, an Indian woman came by (we were near the territory of the Creek nation); she was leading by the hand a little white girl of five or six, whom I presumed to be the daughter of the pioneer. A Negro woman followed them. There was about the dress of the Indian woman some native grandeur: rings of metal were hanging from her ears and nostrils; her hair, woven with glass beads, fell freely on her shoulders, and I saw that she was not married, for she wore the shell necklace that virgins customarily set on their nuptial bed; the Negro woman was dressed in ragged European clothes.

All three came to sit beside the spring, and the young savage, taking the child in her arms, covered her with caresses such as one would expect to burst from the heart of a mother; the Negro woman, for her part, sought by a variety of innocent games to attract the attention of the little Creole girl. In her every movement, the child displayed a sentiment of superiority that was in strange contrast with her young age; one would have said that she somehow condescended to accept the attentions of her companions.

The Negro woman, crouching before her mistress and attending to her every wish, seemed equally torn between an almost maternal attachment and servile fear; while even in the tender effusiveness of the Indian there was an air of freedom and an almost fierce pride.

I approached and watched this spectacle in silence; my curiosity must have annoyed the Indian woman, for she rose suddenly, pushed the child away from her abruptly, and after giving me an angry glance, disappeared into the woods.

It often happened that I would see together in one place individuals belonging to the three races that inhabit North America; I had already noticed a thousand different examples of the dominance of the whites; but in the scene I have just described, something particularly moving was apparent: a bond of affection bringing together the oppressed and the oppressor, and their coming together in nature made all the more striking the immense distance that laws and prejudice had thrown between them.

Volume II

PREFACE

In America, democratic social conditions have naturally recommended certain laws and political mores.

Moreover, this social order has given birth to a great many sentiments and opinions that were unknown in the old aristocratic societies of Europe. It has broken down or altered the relationships that existed previously, and created new ones. The face of civil society has changed just as much as that of the political world.

I addressed the first topic in my work on American democracy published five years ago. The second topic is the subject of the present book. These two parts supplement each other and form a single work.

I must first caution the reader against an assumption that would do me a disservice.

Noting that I attribute so many different results to social equality, the reader could conclude that I regard equality as the sole cause of everything happening today. That interpretation assumes a very narrow view on my part.

Today many opinions, attitudes, and feelings originated in conditions unrelated to equality and even quite contrary to it. That is why, if we take the United States as an example, I might easily demonstrate that, quite independently of democratic social conditions, the nature of the country, the origins of its inhabitants, the religion of the first founders, the education they acquired, their previous habits, have all had and continue to have an immense influence on the way they think and feel. Different causes, also quite apart from equal conditions, are found in Europe and would explain a great part of what is happening there.

I recognize the existence of all these different causes and their importance, but it is not my purpose to address them. I have not undertaken to show the reasons for all our inclinations and all our ideas; I have chosen to show only how democracy has shaped them all.

Given the fact that I strongly believe the democratic revolution we are witnessing today is irresistible and that it would be neither desirable nor wise to resist, it may be surprising that, in this book, I have frequently written harsh words about the democratic societies created by this revolution.

I would reply simply that it is because I was not in any way an enemy of democracy that I have tried to be honest about it.

People do not like to hear the truth from their enemies, and their friends rarely offer it; that is why I have spoken out.

I believed that many people would come forth to proclaim all the good that equality promised to mankind, but that very few would dare to point out from afar the dangers threatening it. Thus it was primarily to those dangers that I turned my attention, and, believing that I saw them clearly, I would not remain silent from cowardice.

I hope that readers will find in this second volume the same impartiality that was noted in the first. Situated between the contradictory views that divide us, I have attempted for the moment to erase from my heart both the favorable and unfavorable feelings that each of them evokes in me. If readers of my book find in it a single phrase meant to flatter any one of the great parties agitating our country, or a single one of the smaller factions that plague and weaken it, let him speak up and blame me openly.

The subject that I have taken on is immense; it includes most of the feelings and ideas that the new state of the world engenders. Such a subject is beyond my abilities; I am not at all satisfied that I have succeeded.

However, if I have not achieved everything I have attempted, readers will at least grant that I conceived and attempted the enterprise in a spirit to make me worthy of success.

Part I: The Influence of Democracy upon the Intellectual Development of the United States

[. . .]

CHAPTER 11

The Principal Source of Beliefs among Democratic Countries

Doctrinal beliefs increase and decrease over time. They spring up in different ways and may take different forms and objects; without them mankind would be lost, for dogmatic beliefs are the received opinions men accept confidently and without argument. If everyone set about forming all of his views on his own, and pursued his own path to truth in isolation, it is unlikely that very many men would ever agree on a single common belief.

It is clear that no society can prosper without shared beliefs, or rather, none that can long endure; for without shared ideas, there is no communal action, and without communal actions, there are individuals but no society. For society to exist, and more importantly to prosper, there must be some principal ideas that bring people together and hold them together ideologically; and that cannot happen unless each of them sometimes draws his views from a single source and agrees to accept certain attitudes fully formed.

Turning next to consider men individually, I find that dogmatic beliefs are no less important for living alone than they are for common action among peers.

If man had to prove for himself the truths he depends on every day, he would never finish; he would bog down in preliminaries without ever getting anywhere; no one has the time, given the brevity of life, or the ability, given the limitations of the mind, to do it; men must accept on faith a whole raft of facts and opinions that he has had neither leisure nor ability to examine and verify on his own, but that

---

Chapter 11 appeared as Volume II, Part I, Chapter 2 in the original, complete text.

more talented men have discovered or that the populace has adopted. This is the initial foundation upon which he constructs the framework for his own thoughts. He does not do this from personal preference; an unyielding law of the human condition forces it upon him.

There is no great philosopher in the world who does not take on faith a thousand things from others, and who does not accept the truth of things he has not personally established.

This is not only necessary but desirable. An individual who attempted to examine everything by himself could devote little time and attention to every detail; the effort would keep his mind in a state of perpetual unease and would prevent him from penetrating deeply into a single truth or establishing with certainty a single fact. His intelligence would be both independent and weak; given all the different objects of human opinions, it is essential for an individual to make a choice and adopt some beliefs without questioning them, in order to go deeper into a small number that he reserves for examination.

It is true that anyone who accepts an opinion based on someone else's word subjugates his own mind; but it is a salutary servitude that allows him to make better use of freedom.

Consequently, whatever the circumstances, intellectual and moral authority must reside somewhere. Its location may change, but it must have a place. The degree of individual independence may vary, but it cannot be unlimited. Thus, the question is not whether intellectual authority exists in democratic times, but simply where it is to be found and how much of it there is.

I [have already] indicated that equality of condition has given men a kind of instinctive incredulity about anything supernatural, and a very great, and sometimes exaggerated, notion about human rationality.

Thus it is difficult to persuade men living in these times of equality to submit to any intellectual authority outside and above humanity. They look for the ordinary sources of truth within themselves or their peers. That alone should prove that no new religion can arise during these times, and that all attempts to bring them into being would be not only impious but also ridiculous and unreasonable. Predictably, a democratic people will not easily believe in a divine mission, will laugh at new prophets, and will look for the principal arbiter of beliefs within humanity and not without.

When conditions are unequal and people are dissimilar, there will be a few very educated, wise individuals with powerful intellects, and a multitude of ignorant and limited ones. Those living in times of aristocracy are naturally inclined to look to the superior reason of an individual or a class for opinions, and be less inclined to recognize the infallibility of the masses.

In centuries of equality, the opposite is true.

As citizens become more equal and more similar, the tendency of anyone to believe blindly in a single person or class diminishes. The inclination to believe in the masses grows, and increasingly that opinion prevails in the world.

Not only is popular opinion the only guide to individual reason among democratic people, but it has an infinitely greater influence there than it has elsewhere. In times of equality, men lack faith in each other because of their similarities; but this same similarity gives them an almost unlimited confidence in the judgment of the public; it is not conceivable to them that, as they are all similarly enlightened, the truth could be found anywhere but on the side of the majority.

When a man living in a democratic country compares himself to those around him, he feels proudly that he is the equal of anyone; but when he pictures his peers as a group and puts himself alongside the people as a whole, he is also overwhelmed by his own insignificance and his weakness.

That same equality that renders him independent from any one of his fellow citizens also exposes his isolation and defenselessness before the actions of the majority.

So the public, in democratic countries, has a singular strength that aristocratic nations could not begin to imagine. It does not use persuasion to impose its beliefs, it implants them and penetrates the soul through the force of public pressure on the intellect of the individual.

In the United States the majority expects to provide the individual with a host of ready-made opinions, thus relieving them of the obligation to form their own. There are a great many theories in the field of philosophy, whether moral or political, that everyone adopts on faith without examination; and if you look closely, you will see that religion there is accepted less as revealed doctrine than as public opinion.

I know that, among Americans, political laws are such that the majority rules society absolutely; this greatly increases the power it wields over thought. There is nothing more natural than for men to recognize superior wisdom in their oppressors.

The political omnipotence of the majority in the United States adds to the influence that public opinion has on the minds of individuals but it is not the source of it. We must look for the sources of this influence in equality itself, and not in the more or less popular institutions that egalitarian people provide for themselves. It may be that the intellectual grip of the majority would be less absolute among a democratic people living under a king than in the heart of a pure democracy; but it will always be absolute, and, whatever the political laws that govern men in times of equality, we can predict that faith in popular opinion will become a sort of religion whose prophet will be the people.

Intellectual authority will therefore be different, but it will not decline; and far from believing that it must disappear, I predict that it will quickly become too great and that it could eventually restrict individual reason within even narrower limits than is adequate for the greatness and happiness of mankind. I definitely see in equality two tendencies: one that could move the mind of each individual to new ways of thinking, and the other that would reduce him to the point of choosing not to think at all. And I also see how, under the sway of certain laws, democracy may extinguish the very intellectual liberty that social democracy favors so that after having broken all the shackles that certain classes or individuals once imposed, the human spirit will be stifled by the general will of the majority.

If, in place of the various excessive powers that have impeded or slowed the thrust of individual reason, democratic people simply substitute the absolute power of a majority, only the character of evil would have changed. Men would not have found a means for living independently; sadly, they would have found merely a new face for servitude. I cannot say it strongly enough: that should give all those for whom freedom of thought is sacred and who hate not the despot but despotism something to think about very seriously. For my part, when I feel the hand of power pressing on my brow, I care little about who is oppressing me, and I am not more willing to bend my head to the yoke simply because it is offered by a million arms. [. . .]

CHAPTER 12

The Spirit in Which Americans Cultivate the Arts

I would consider it a waste of my own and the reader's time to try to prove that modest wealth, the absence of luxury, the universal desire for prosperity, and the unceasing effort on the part of everyone to acquire it lead men to prefer the practical above the beautiful. Democratic nations, in which all these qualities converge, will of course cultivate arts that help make life more comfortable in preference to those whose sole purpose is to be beautiful; they will invariably prefer the practical to the beautiful, and they will want the beautiful to be useful.

I intend to do more than this, and, after having shown the former quality, to describe several others.

Ordinarily, during periods of aristocracy, the exercise of almost all the arts becomes a privilege and every profession is a world of its own into which not everyone is entitled to enter. Moreover, even when industry is free, the natural immobility of aristocratic nations means that ultimately all those engaged in the same field form a distinct class, comprising always the same families, and all of whose members know each other, and who quickly come to share a common identity and pride. In this type of industrial class, every artisan not only has to make a living, but also to protect his reputation. He is not simply motivated by his own and his customers' interests but also by the interest of his craft, and it is in the interest of the craft that every artisan produces masterpieces. In periods of aristocracy, the aim of the arts is thus to produce objects of the highest quality, not the highest quantity at the lowest cost.

In contrast, when every profession is open to anyone, when the mob comes and goes endlessly, and when the various members are strangers to each other, indifferent and almost invisible because of their numbers, the social ties are broken and every worker, relying only on himself, strives only to earn as much as possible with the lowest cost; he is limited only by the will of the consumer; during this time, the consumer undergoes a corresponding revolution.

In countries where wealth, like power, is concentrated in the hands of a few and stays there, the use of most worldly goods belongs to a small number of the same people and remains the same; need, attitudes, and moderate desires eliminate other things.

Since this aristocratic class remains static in its superior position, neither shrinking nor expanding, its needs remain the same. People in that class have acquired, given the superior and hereditary position they occupy, a preference for what is well-made and long-lasting.

This gives a certain shape to the nation's ideas about art.

Often among such people, even the peasant will prefer to do without the things he desires than to acquire inferior things.

In aristocracies, workers are producing for a small number of customers who are hard to please. Any profit they make will depend primarily upon the perfection of their goods.

This is no longer the case when, after privileges have been lost, ranks intermingle and everyone moves endlessly up and down the social ladder.

You can always find, in democratic societies, a huge number of citizens whose patrimony has been divided up and diminished. In better times, these people came to expect certain things that they are no longer able to afford, and they are restlessly looking for roundabout ways of attaining them.

Moreover, in democracies there are many people whose fortunes are growing but whose desires are growing even faster and who want things long before they can afford them. They look left and right for shortcuts to these pleasures that seem so close. The result of this combination means that there are always many people in democracies whose needs surpass their resources and who, rather than give up something they desire, will settle for second-best.

The tradesman understands these feelings, because he shares them; in aristocracies, he would aim to sell his things at a high price to only a small number; now he decides that the fastest way to grow rich is to sell cheaply to everyone.

There are two ways to lower the cost of merchandise.

The first is to find the best, fastest, and smartest way to produce goods. The second is to make things in great quantity that are almost as good but of lower value. Among democratic societies, a worker puts all of his thinking into these two pursuits.

He strains to invent processes that will allow him to work not better but faster and with lower costs, and, if he can't do that, to lower the intrinsic qualities of the object he is making, without making it entirely unsuitable for the purpose for which it is intended. When only the rich had watches, they almost all were excellent. Now, only mediocre watches are made, but everyone owns one. Thus, not only does democracy tend to direct the human spirit to the useful arts, it encourages artisans to make a lot of imperfect things very fast, and persuades the consumer to settle for them.

I do not mean that art in democracies is incapable of producing marvels when called on to do so. They appear occasionally, when a buyer agrees to pay for the time and effort. In this struggle between all industries, in the midst of immense competition and countless experiments, there are some excellent craftsmen who have attained the pinnacle of their profession. But they rarely have a chance to show what they are capable of doing; they carefully conserve their efforts and knowingly maintain a self-monitoring mediocrity; capable of going far beyond this standard, they aim low. By contrast, in aristocratic societies, workers produced only the best they were capable of, and when they stopped, it was only when they reached the limits of knowledge.

When I arrive in a country and notice that artists have produced some beautiful objects, I learn nothing about the social and political makeup of the country. However, if I observe that the works of art are generally imperfect, abundant, and cheap, I know that there are few people of privilege and a mixing of classes, which will soon disappear entirely.

Artisans who live in democratic societies not only attempt to put their practical goods within reach of everyone, they are still attempting to give all their products some brilliant qualities that these do not have.

When social classes mix, everyone tries to appear to be something he is not and makes a great effort to do so. Democracy does not create this feeling, which is simply part of human nature; but it does apply it to material goods; hypocrisy of virtue is typical of every age; hypocrisy of wealth belongs particularly to democratic eras.

The arts will resort to any kind of forgery to meet the current needs of human vanity; industry goes so far in this that it is becoming self-destructive. We are already at the point where diamonds are so well imitated that it is easy to be misled. As soon as the art of making fake diamonds is invented, such that it is impossible to distinguish the real from the fake, both will be rejected, and they will become again like stones.

This leads me to speak of those arts we have come to call, *par excellence*, fine arts.

I do not believe that the decline in the number of people who pursue the fine arts is necessarily the result of democratic social conditions and institutions, but they will have a powerful influence on the manner in which the fine arts are cultivated. As most of those who have already acquired a taste for the fine arts have grown poorer, and on the other side, most of those who are not yet rich are beginning to aspire, through imitation, to fine art, the number of consumers generally increases, while rich and discriminating consumers decline. We will begin to see in the fine arts something analogous to what I have already described about the useful arts: the value of a work will decline as the quantity increases.

No longer striving for what is great, people will seek the elegant and the beautiful; appearance will mean more than substance.

In aristocracies, a few great paintings are produced, and in democratic societies, a lot of minor ones. In the first, bronze statues are erected, and in the second, plaster statues are poured.

When I arrived in New York for the first time from the Atlantic Ocean via the East River, I was surprised to see, all along the banks, a number of small villas of white marble at some distance from the city, built in the old style of architecture; the next day, after going to look more closely at the ones that were most remarkable, I found that the walls were of brick painted white and the columns were painted wood. It was the same for all the buildings I had admired the day before.

Democratic conditions and institutions also give to all the arts of imitation certain specific tendencies that are easily noticed. They often avoid paintings of the soul in favor of those of the body; and they replace representations of movement and feeling with emotion and ideology; in other words, they substitute the real for the ideal.

CHAPTER 13

Literary Production

Not only does democracy affect the literary taste of the industrial classes, it also introduces an industrial spirit into literature.

In aristocracies, readers are demanding and few in number; in democracies, they are numerous and more easily satisfied. The result is that a writer may hope for success in aristocracy only through great effort, and this effort, which may lead to glory, will not necessarily be lucrative; but in democratic societies, a writer may brag of acquiring both fame and fortune at little cost. It is enough to be popular, not necessarily admired.

The ever-growing throng of readers and their continual need for something new assures that even a book they do not appreciate will sell.

In democracies, the public often treats writers the way kings once did their courtiers: they are well paid, but despised. What more can corrupt souls expect, whether they were born at court or simply worthy of living there?

Chapter 13 appeared as Volume II, Part I, Chapter 14 in the original, complete text.

Democratic literature is crawling with authors who see in writing simply a trade, and for every great writer, there are thousands of idea peddlers.

CHAPTER 14

Certain Characteristics of Historians in Democratic Centuries

Historians writing in aristocratic centuries generally ascribed all events to the will of an individual and the attitudes of certain men, and they were quick to attach revolutionary importance to the slightest accidents. Wisely, they grasped the minor causes and often overlooked the major ones.

Historians living in democratic centuries tend to do just the opposite.

Most of them attribute to individuals almost no influence over the destiny of mankind, or to citizens any influence over the fate of society. However, they do grasp the broad general causes behind particular, minor details. There is an explanation for these differences.

When historians in aristocratic centuries look over the world theater, the first thing they see is a very small number of main players running the entire show. These great individuals, who are permanently front and center on the stage capture their attention and hold it: while they attempt to discover the private motives of these few characters, they overlook the rest.

The importance of the things they see a few men doing gives them an exaggerated idea of the influence one man can have and inclines them naturally to believe that the explanation of the movements of the many is always to be found in the actions of a single individual.

When, by contrast, all citizens are dependent upon one another and when each of them is weak, there appears to be no one who has much control at all, and certainly not lasting control, over the mass of humanity. At first glance, individuals seem to be helpless over the mass of citizens, and it appears that society moves on its own with the free and willing support of everyone in it.

Chapter 14 appeared as Volume II, Part I, Chapter 20 in the original, complete text.

That leads us to reflect on the overall explanation for why so many minds simultaneously turn in a similar direction.

I am quite convinced that, within a democratic nation itself, the mentality, the vices or virtues of certain individuals can impede or advance the natural course of the nation's destiny; but such secondary and fortuitous causes are infinitely more varied, more hidden, more complex, less potent, and consequently more difficult to discern and to trace in times of equality than in aristocratic centuries, when one has only to analyze, among all the general facts, the acts of a single individual or very few.

A historian would quickly tire of such work; his mind would wander in that labyrinth, and, unable to make anything out very clearly and to bring to light enough individual influences, he would deny that they exist. He prefers to tell us about the nature of races, the physical makeup of a country, or the spirit of civilization. That simplifies his work and at the very least, is more satisfying for the reader.

M. de La Fayette wrote somewhere in his Memoires that the exaggerated system of general causes is tremendously satisfying for mediocre public personages. I would add that it is quite the same for mediocre historians. It gives them a few sweeping causes that promptly relieve them of the most difficult part of their book and encourages weak or lazy minds, while making them appear profound.

For myself, I think in every period some events of this world must be attributed to very general causes, and others to more specific ones. These two types of causes are always present; they differ only in degree. Generalizations explain more during democratic centuries than during aristocratic ones, and specific causes less. In aristocratic times, the opposite is true: particular causes are given more importance, and general causes less, unless one regards inequality of conditions as a general cause, since then some individuals are able to thwart the natural inclinations of many.

Historians who seek to portray what happens in democratic societies are thus correct in giving a greater role to general causes, and in working to find them; but they are mistaken in denying entirely the particular acts of individuals simply because that is hard to see and to trace.

Not only are historians in democratic times inclined to find sweeping explanations for every event, but they are also likely to fold facts into each other and to derive from them a system.

In aristocratic centuries, historians' attention is always focused on the individual, the sequence of events escapes them, or they simply do not acknowledge that there is a sequence. The fabric of history seems to them constantly unwoven by the passage of a particular person.

In democratic centuries, however, historians, seeing less the agents and more the acts, easily recognize a relationship and methodical order connecting them.

Ancient literature, which has left us such beautiful histories, offers almost no great historical systems, whereas even the most minor modern ones are teeming with them. It seems that ancient historians made no use of those general theories that those of today always risk abusing.

Writers in democratic centuries run another risk, as well.

When the evidence of individuals' actions on society is lost, it often looks as if the world is moving without a mover. Because it is difficult to perceive and analyze the forces that, acting separately on the will of each citizen, end up causing movement, one is tempted to believe that this movement is not voluntary and that societies unknowingly obey some superior force that shapes them.

Even if we were to discover on earth the general law directing the individual will of all people, that would not rescue human freedom. A law vast enough to apply at one time to millions of men, and strong enough to incline them all to a single purpose may well be irresistible; when we see people ceding to it, we begin to think society is incapable of resisting.

Historians who live in democratic times do not simply deny that some citizens are capable of influencing the destiny of a country, they deny that the people themselves have the power to change their own destiny, and they subject them either to an inflexible providence, or to blind fatalism. According to these historians, each nation is unalterably bound by its geography, its founding, its forefathers, and its character, to a particular destiny that no effort could alter. They consider all generations as united and going back in this way, from age to age and from one inexorable event to another, to the beginning of the world; they find one long and solid chain wrapping around the entire human race, binding it.

But describing how things came to be is not enough; they want to show that they could not have happened in any other way. They look at a nation at a particular place in its history and insist that it came there by the only path open to it. It is easier to say that than to explain what it might have done to find a better route.

Reading the historians of aristocratic ages and particularly those of antiquity, it seems that a man had only to become master of himself to be master of his own destiny and to rule others. To read the histories written today, one would conclude that man is powerless over himself as well as those around him. Ancient historians taught leadership, those of our day teach only obedience. In their books, the author looks very grand, humanity very weak.

If this doctrine of fatality, so appealing to those who write history in democratic times, were to pass from the writers to their readers, penetrating the citizenry as a whole, and were to take hold in public opinion, the day could come when new social movements would be paralyzed and Christian nations be reduced to the status of Turks.

Moreover, I think that such a doctrine is particularly dangerous in our own time; our contemporaries are only too inclined to doubt free will: they feel limited by individual weakness, but they are still ready to acknowledge the power and independence of men united as a social group. We must not let this idea fade, for it is important to raise men's spirits, not beat them down completely.

Part II: Influence of Democracy on the Opinions of Americans

CHAPTER 15

Individualism in Democratic Society

I have explained how, during periods of equality, everyone looked for beliefs within himself; I wish now to show how it is, during these same periods, that attitudes are also all directed inwardly.

Individualism is a recent expression that has arisen out of a new concept. Our ancestors knew only of egoism.

Egoism is a passionate and exaggerated love of oneself, and leads a man to think only of himself, and to prefer himself to everyone else.

Individualism is a reflective and quiet sentiment that inclines each individual to distance himself from a crowd of peers and to draw apart with his own family and friends; in this way he builds his own private world, willingly leaving the larger world to itself.

Chapter 15 appeared as Volume II, Part II, Chapter 2 in the original, complete text.

Egoism is born of blind instinct; individualism proceeds from erroneous judgment rather than depraved character. It springs from a weakness of spirit rather than vices of the heart.

Egoism dries up the seeds of every virtue, whereas individualism begins simply by sapping public virtues; over the long run, however, it attacks and destroys all the others and ultimately is absorbed into egoism.

Egoism is a vice as old as the world. It belongs no more to one form of society than to another.

Individualism springs from democracy, and it threatens to increase as conditions of equality increase.

In aristocratic societies, families remain in the same position and often in the same place for centuries. That means, generally, that all generations are contemporaries. A man will almost always know and respect his ancestors; he thinks about his great-grandchildren, and loves them. He willingly fulfills his responsibilities to all of them, and frequently sacrifices his personal desires to those who are not yet born, or who are no longer alive.

Aristocratic institutions have the effect of closely linking everyone to many fellow citizens.

As classes are quite distinct and immobile within aristocratic society, each class becomes a world within a world for everyone who belongs to it, more familiar and beloved than the larger one.

Since all citizens in an aristocratic society have a permanent place, one above the other, each one recognizes someone above him whose protection he needs, and below him sees someone else to whom he can turn for support.

Consequently, people living in aristocratic societies are usually very closely linked to something outside themselves, and they are prepared at times to forget about themselves. Of course the very notion of human fellowship is vague during such periods and one would hardly think of devoting himself to the cause of mankind; yet he would often sacrifice himself for another individual.

In democratic societies, however, in which every individual's duty to his fellow man is clear, devotion to an individual is rare; the bonds of human affection grow strained, and loosen.

Among democratic peoples, new families constantly come out of nowhere, while others fall into obscurity, and the ones remaining change their appearance; the fabric of the ages is being torn all the time, and the traces of past generations are erased. People naturally forget about those who preceded them, and have no notion about those who will follow. They are concerned only for the ones closest to them.

As all the classes come closer together and merge, their members change and become strangers to each other. Aristocracy once formed a long chain that linked everyone from peasant to king; democracy breaks that chain and separates every link.

As social equality expands, there are a great many people who, neither rich enough nor powerful enough to have much influence with their peers, have nevertheless acquired or held onto enough education and property to be self-sufficient. They owe nothing to anyone, they expect nothing from anyone; they are accustomed to thinking of themselves as solitary, and naturally they assume that destiny is in their own hands.

Democracy, therefore, not only makes a man forget his ancestors, but it conceals his descendents and separates him from his contemporaries; it turns him back upon himself forever and threatens to shut him off entirely in the solitude of his own heart.

CHAPTER 16

Individualism Is Greater Following a Democratic Revolution Than in Any Other Period

It is precisely at the moment when a democratic society has emerged out of the ruins of aristocracy that the isolation separating men and its ensuing egoism is most obvious to an observer.

Not only do these societies include a large number of independent citizens, they are filling up daily with people who, having only just achieved independence, are drunk on their newly acquired power; these men have a presumptuous notion of their own strength, and, never imagining that they might one day need to call on their peers for support, provide ample evidence that they are thinking only of themselves.

For the most part, aristocracies fall only after a prolonged struggle, during which implacable hatred is enflamed between the different

---

Chapter 16 appeared as Volume II, Part II, Chapter 3 in the original, complete text.

classes. These passions survive beyond the battle, and we see traces of them in the democratic confusion that follows.

Those citizens who were previously first in the hierarchy do not immediately forget their former greatness; for a long time they consider themselves strangers within the new society. They have scant interest in the fate of those whom society has made their equals and whom they regard as oppressors. They have lost sight of their former peers and no longer feel connected to them by a shared destiny; everyone draws apart, feeling that he need only take care of himself. Those who were once at the bottom of the social ladder, however, and whom revolution has suddenly put on an equal footing, find their pleasure in their newly acquired independence mixed with concealed anxiety; when they meet, they look in triumph and fear upon those they once regarded as socially superior, then go their separate ways.

So from the very start, citizens in democratic societies are inclined to isolate themselves.

Democracy leads men to keep their distance from each other; and democratic revolutions tend to make them avoid each other, perpetuating among equals the hatreds that grew out of inequality.

The great advantage of the Americans is that they came to democracy without having suffered a democratic revolution; equals from birth, they did not become equals later.

CHAPTER 17

Americans Minimize Individualism with Free Institutions

Despotism, fearful by nature, considers the isolation of individuals as the best guarantee of its own survival, and typically does its best to encourage it. No vice of the human heart is more supportive of despotism than egotism; a despot readily forgives his subjects for failing to love him as long as they don't love each other. He does not ask their help in governing and is satisfied as long as they make no claim to govern themselves. He considers restless and disruptive those who wish to work together for the common good, and, transforming the natural meaning of the words, he considers good citizens to be those who shut themselves off.

As a result, the vices despotism breeds are the very ones favored by equality. These two complement and nurture each other in dangerous ways.

Equality places men side by side without common bonds to hold them together. Despotism raises barriers between them and separates them. It gives them little reason to think of one another and it makes an attitude of indifference a public virtue.

Despotism is dangerous in every age, and so is particularly threatening during democratic eras.

Obviously at such times men have a particular need of liberty.

When citizens are required to concern themselves with public affairs, they are necessarily drawn away from their private interests and, on occasion, forced to notice others.

When men must work communally for the common good, they see that they are not as independent of their fellow citizens as first thought, and for their mutual benefit they must support each other.

When the public governs, everyone recognizes the value of public approval and seeks to earn the respect and good will of those among whom he must live and work.

Some of the emotions that make men coldhearted and drive them apart have to be suppressed and hidden. Pride must be disguised; scorn dare not reveal itself. Egotism itself is intimidated.

In a free government most public servants are elected and men who are driven by high-minded motives or restless ambition find private life too confining and are unable to ignore the people all around them.

Sometimes ambition motivates a man to serve others, and he benefits when he sets aside his own needs. I know that there are some who will remind me of all the intrigues that elections create, the shameful tactics candidates often use, and the lies spread by their enemies. These are opportunities for feuds and they occur more and more often as elections become more frequent.

These are great evils, of course, but they are temporary, whereas the benefits that result endure.

The desire to win election may lead some men into a momentary conflict; but in the long run the same desire leads men to help each other; and, although an election may by chance come between friends, the electoral system permanently brings together a great many more who would have remained strangers to each other. Liberty creates intense hatreds, but despotism leads to general indifference.

Americans have successfully overcome the individualism engendered by equality with liberty.

American founders believed that giving self-representation to the nation as a whole was not enough to guard against a malady that, though natural to society in a democratic age, was still dangerous; they saw fit to allow for political action in each region of the country, ensuring countless opportunities for citizens to act in concert and to remind them daily of their dependence upon each other.

This was very wise.

The nationwide affairs of a country concern only the leaders. They meet together only from time to time; and, since they frequently lose touch following these meetings, they do not establish lasting bonds. However, when the citizens of a particular region must deal with regional concerns, the same individuals are in daily contact and are more or less obliged to get to know each other and get along.

It is always difficult to interest individuals in state government because they have trouble grasping the meaning in their own lives. But when a road has to be built along someone's property, he sees immediately the impact of this small public project on his larger personal concerns and realizes without being told the close connection between private and public interests.

It is when citizens are given responsibility for administering local affairs as opposed to national ones that they become concerned for the public good and recognize that they must support each other in order to achieve it.

It is possible to win popular favor through a single heroic act; however, the love and respect of the people is earned through a lifetime of service, of good deeds, and of habitual goodwill, and through an established reputation for unselfish action.

Local freedoms ensure that a great many people value the goodwill of their friends and neighbors, and by bringing them together constantly forces them to meet and compromise.

In the United States, the wealthiest citizens are always careful not to distance themselves from the people; instead, they meet constantly, are willing to listen and speak together every day. They know that in a democracy the rich always need the poor and that, in democratic societies one appeals to the poor more through behavior than through good deeds. In fact, the very size of good deeds, highlighting the difference in status, is the source of a hidden irritation to their beneficiaries; simplicity of manners, however, has an irresistible charm: familiarity is appealing and even their coarseness is not always objectionable.

This truth does not always penetrate the minds of the wealthy right away. They usually resist throughout the democratic revolution and they do not even see it immediately afterward. They willingly agree to work for the good of the people, but they wish to continue to keep their distance. They believe that that is enough, but they are mistaken. They will fail miserably if they are unable to win the hearts of the people around them. What they are called upon to give up is their pride, not their money.

It is said that the imaginative Americans are constantly inventing ways of increasing wealth and meeting public needs. The greatest minds in every region are engaged in discovering hidden new ways of increasing the common prosperity; once they find them, they quickly make them public.

Observing closely the weaknesses and vices frequently found among those in government makes the growing prosperity of the people seem at first surprising. It should not. Elected leaders of government do not produce the prosperity of American democracy; America prospers because its leaders are elected.

It would be a mistake to think that the patriotism of Americans and the zeal that everyone feels for the general good are not genuine. Although self-interest in the United States, as elsewhere, drives most human endeavor, it is not the only motivation.

I must say that I have seen Americans make substantial, real sacrifices in public affairs, and I have noticed hundreds of times that, when necessary, they almost never fail to show their loyalty to one another.

The free institutions belonging to all the people of the United States, and the political rights they so freely exercise, remind every citizen constantly, and in countless ways, that he lives in society with others. He is always mindful of the idea that it is both a duty and a benefit to be of use to others; and, as he has no particular reason to hate them, because he is neither slave nor master, his heart is inclined to demonstrate his goodwill. Concern for the general good is first a necessity and then a choice; what was calculated becomes instinctive; and, by dint of working for the good of others, one acquires both a habit and a preference for service.

Many people in France consider social equality as the greatest evil and political freedom as the second greatest. When they are obliged to endure one, they strive to escape at least the other. I myself believe that political freedom is the only remedy for the evils produced by equality.

CHAPTER 18

The Role of Voluntary Associations in America

I am not interested now in political associations that serve as a defense against either the despotism of the majority or the encroachments of royal power. They were addressed previously. It is clear that as individual citizens become weaker and less capable of preserving their freedoms, equality will lead to greater tyranny unless each individual learns the art of joining with others to defend freedom. My concern here is strictly with the growth of civil associations that do not have a political purpose.

Political associations are only one part of the vast number of associations in the United States.

Americans of all ages and stations, all points of view, meet constantly. Not only do they belong to commercial and industrial associations, but there are countless others: religious and moral, serious and futile, some very broad and others very specific, large and small; Americans gather to celebrate holidays, establish seminaries, build inns, erect churches, distribute books, and send missionaries to the far corners of the world; this is how they build hospitals, prisons, and schools. Whether it is a matter of spreading information or making an appeal for public support, they form associations. Wherever you would expect to find a new enterprise led by government, as in France, or by a highborn lord, as in England, in the United States you will find an association taking the lead.

In America I encountered associations that I confess I had never even imagined, and I have often admired the endless creativity of the people of the United States in managing to unite a large number of people behind a common effort, who voluntarily move it forward.

Chapter 18 appeared as Volume II, Part II, Chapter 5 in the original, complete text.

I have looked all over England, from which some American laws and many customs were drawn, and it seemed to me that there was nothing like the same efficient and constant use of associations there.

It often happens that the English achieve very great things working alone, whereas there is hardly any undertaking, no matter how small, that Americans do not do in associations. It is evident that the English may consider associations as a powerful means of action but Americans view them as the only way to proceed.

The most democratic country on earth is therefore the one in which men have most nearly perfected the art of joining their efforts in the pursuit of common goals and have applied this new art to the greatest number of projects. Is this accidental, or might there actually be a connection between associations and equality?

At the center of aristocratic societies there exists a multitude of individuals who can do nothing on their own, and a small number of powerful and rich citizens, each of whom can accomplish great things alone.

In aristocratic societies, men have no need to join together to act because they are so closely bound to each other. Every wealthy and powerful citizen automatically serves as the head of some kind of permanent association consisting of all those who depend upon him and who must compete to carry out his plans.

In democratic societies, however, all citizens are weak and independent; they can accomplish almost nothing alone, and no one can oblige anyone else to do anything. Unless they learn to cooperate freely, they are helpless.

If men living in democratic countries had neither the right nor the desire to unite to achieve their political goals, their independence might be threatened, but they would retain their property and their ideas; however, without the early development of a habit of working together in their daily lives, their very civilization would be in danger. A society in which individuals have lost the capacity to accomplish tasks independently and who then fail to develop the ability to work together for the common good would soon decline, becoming less than civilized.

Unfortunately, the same conditions that make associations so necessary for people in democracy also make them more problematic than elsewhere.

When several members of an aristocracy wish to form an association, they can easily do so. Because each of them has considerable authority in the society, the number of members can be small, and, when members are few, it is easy for them to know and understand each other and to agree to fixed rules.

The same cannot be said of democratic countries, where associations must be large in order to exercise power.

I know that many of my contemporaries are not bothered by this. They claim that if citizens are weak and impotent, government must become competent and active, so that the country can accomplish what individuals cannot. To them, that is sufficient. In this I believe they are wrong.

Government can take the place of some of the largest American associations, and several states in the Union have already tried to do so. But what government could ever provide for the countless small undertakings that American citizens accomplish every day through their associations?

It is easy to imagine the day when people will be less and less able to provide for their most basic and essential needs. The burden on the governing authority will grow without cease, and the scope of the effort will make it ever more vast. The more responsibility it assumes in the place of associations, the more individuals, losing the habit of association, will need and demand: these are causes and effects that keep on building. Will the public authority end up running everything that a single citizen cannot handle? And if the time comes, as a consequence of the constant division of property, shared endlessly so that it can no longer be cultivated except by a labor association, will the head of state have to abandon the helm and take up the plow?

The morale and spirit of a democratic people would risk nothing less than their very enterprise and productivity if government were to replace associations in everything.

Feelings and ideas do not renew themselves, the heart cannot grow or the human mind expand except through interaction with others.

I have shown that there is almost no such reciprocal activity in democracy. Thus it must be produced artificially and this is what associations alone are able to provide.

When members of an aristocracy adopt a new idea or embrace a new sensibility, they place them as it were on the same pedestal they themselves occupy and thus expose them to the view of all; their ideas are easily introduced into the hearts and minds of the people around them.

In democratic countries, only government is naturally capable of doing this, but it is easy to see that government action is never enough and often dangerous.

A government could no more sustain and renew the flow of feelings and ideas of the people than it could run all the industrial enterprises. Once it steps outside the political sphere to start down this new path, it becomes, unintentionally, intolerably repressive; for government can only rule through precise laws; it imposes the attitudes and ideas it favors; its advice is not easily distinguished from its orders.

This would be even worse if it actually believed that stability was best. Then it would remain static and allow itself to sink into lethargy.

Therefore, it must not act alone.

In democratic society, associations are needed to replace the powerful individuals eliminated by equality.

Once a few people in the United States conceive a sentiment or an idea that they wish to develop in the world, they seek each other out and they have a meeting. At that point, they cease to be isolated individuals and become a far-reaching power able to serve as an example: when they speak, people listen.

The first time I heard that there were a hundred thousand men in the United States who had publicly vowed to avoid hard liquor, I did not take it seriously, but as a joke. At first I could not see why these very temperate citizens did not simply agree to drink water at home.

In the end I understood that these hundred thousand Americans, worried about the increasing drunkenness all around, wanted to support the cause of sobriety. They had acted exactly as a nobleman might, dressing plainly in order to inspire scorn for ostentation among the common people. If these hundred thousand men had lived in France, we can be sure that each of them would have appealed individually to the government to call for greater supervision of bars throughout the realm.

There is nothing, in my view, that merits our attention more than these intellectual and moral associations in America. Political and industrial associations are readily apparent, but the others escape our notice, and when we do see them, they perplex us because we have almost nothing analogous to them. We ought to acknowledge, however, that the latter are just as important to Americans as the former, and perhaps even more so.

In democratic countries, knowledge of associations ranks above all knowledge; progress in anything depends upon their progress.

Among the laws that rule human societies, there is one that seems more precise and clear than all the others. For men to remain civilized or to become so, they must develop and perfect the art of association in direct proportion with the growth of equality.

CHAPTER 19

The Relationship between Associations and Newspapers

When people are not firmly and permanently bound to each other, it is difficult for large groups to join together in a common endeavor unless each individual is persuaded that it is in his own interest to do so voluntarily.

That can be done regularly and easily only with the help of newspapers. These supply the only way to put a single idea into thousands of minds at one time.

A newspaper is an immediately accessible adviser; it appears without being sought, and succinctly addresses public issues on a daily basis without interrupting one's personal affairs.

Thus, newspapers become increasingly important as equality expands and the risk of individualism increases. It would be an understatement to say that they simply help to guarantee freedom; they maintain the civilization.

I would not deny that, in democratic countries, newspapers often lead citizens to undertake certain projects together that are very ill-considered; but, if there were no papers, there would be almost no communal activity. The evil they do is much smaller than the evil they cure.

A newspaper is not simply an effective means of suggesting a communal activity to a large number of people; it provides the means for executing plans that they have developed independently.

The leading citizens in aristocratic countries recognize each other across long distances; and, when they wish to join forces, they walk over to each other, leading a multitude of followers.

However, in democratic countries, when a large number of people desire or need to get together, they are often unable to do so because, being few in number and lost in the crowd, they cannot see the others and do not know where to find them. A newspaper article appears presenting a new idea or sentiment that came to each of them simultaneously but independently. It becomes a guiding light for those who had been looking for each other in the darkness and who now are able to meet and unite.

Chapter 19 appeared as Volume II, Part II, Chapter 6 in the original, complete text.

The newspaper brought them together and it continues to be important in keeping them together.

In order for an association to have any power in a democratic society, it must be large. As a result, members are scattered across a vast distance and unable to travel due to limited financial resources and countless responsibilities. They must find a means to communicate every day without seeing each other and to act jointly without meeting. Consequently, there is almost no association that can do without a newspaper.

The connection between associations and newspapers is therefore essential; the newspapers create associations and vice versa; and, if, as I have said, it is true that associations multiply as conditions of equality spread, it is no less true that the number of newspapers should grow in proportion to the number of associations.

And in America one finds the greatest number of associations and the greatest number of newspapers.

This relationship between the number of newspapers and that of associations leads us to discover another between the state of the periodical press in a country and its form of government; we learn that the number of newspapers in a democratic society should increase or decrease in proportion to the degree of administrative centralization. Unlike aristocracies, democratic societies cannot rely upon a few leading citizens to exercise local authority. Their powers must be abolished or spread among a large number of people. Those citizens form an actual association, permanently established by law for the administration of some part of the country, and they need a daily newspaper that reaches them while they work and informs them of the state of affairs in the community. With the growth of local authority, the number of people required by law to exercise that authority grows and with the need for them growing daily, newspapers multiply rapidly.

The extraordinary division of administrative power, much more than the great degree of political freedom and absolute independence of the press, accounts for the singular increase in the number of newspapers in the United States. If all the inhabitants of the Union were able to vote, under rules of a system that limited their voting rights to the selection of the state legislature, they would need no more than a small number of newspapers, because there would be only a few occasions, very important, but rare, that required them to act together; but, within the one great nationwide association, the law has established in every state, every city, and practically every village, small associations for the purpose of local government. The legislative branch therefore requires that every American work together every day, and everyone needs a newspaper for information about the activities of the others.

I believe that a democratic society in which there is no national representation but a large number of small local authorities, would ultimately possess even more newspapers than one in which a centralized administrative power worked alongside an elected legislature. I find that the best explanation for the prodigious spread of a daily press in the United States is the clear combination of the greatest freedom at the national level with local freedoms of every sort.

CHAPTER 20

Connections between Voluntary and Political Associations

There is only one nation in the world in which the unlimited freedom of association is exercised every day for political purposes. This same nation is the only one whose citizens have devised ways to use the right of voluntary association repeatedly in order to achieve all the benefits of their civilization.

In societies where political association is forbidden, voluntary associations are rare. The result is hardly an accidental one and we must conclude that there is a natural and perhaps necessary connection between the two kinds of associations.

People discover their shared interests in a particular issue at random. The matter may involve managing a commercial enterprise or concluding an industrial operation, people meet and join forces, over time they become accustomed to this type of association.

The greater the number of small, shared interests, the more people learn, unconsciously sometimes, the art of working together on large ones.

Voluntary associations make political ones possible; but political associations develop and perfect voluntary associations in a remarkable way.

Chapter 20 appeared as Volume II, Part II, Chapter 7 in the original, complete text.

In civil life, a man knows that, if necessary, he can be self-sufficient. In politics, he would never think so. When society has a public life, the idea of joining together and the desire to form associations present themselves daily to everyone; despite whatever reluctance men have to working together, they will always do so on behalf of a party.

Politics makes associations desirable and customary; it creates the desire for unions and teaches a large number of people who would have lived forever in isolation how to form them.

Politics not only creates a great many associations, it creates enormous ones.

In civil life shared interests seldom attract a common effort on the part of many people automatically. It takes great skill to bring that about.

In politics, the opportunity occurs naturally all the time. It is only in large associations that the real value of the group is apparent. A handful of citizens, individually quite powerless, do not have a clear idea at first of the power they can gain by joining together; they must be shown before they realize it. That is why it is often easier to gather a multitude together than a mere handful; a thousand citizens do not see the value of joining together; ten thousand do. In politics, men join together in large enterprises, and the advantages they derive from large political associations teaches them in a practical way the benefits of working together on small ones.

At the same time, political associations force large numbers of people outside themselves; however far apart they might be in age, attitude, or wealth, politics brings them together and puts them in contact. They meet once and learn to do it again and again.

One cannot join most voluntary associations without risking some assets; it is the same for all industrial and commercial companies. People who are still unfamiliar with the art of associations and who do not understand the basic rules are afraid that the experience of joining together in such a way for the first time will cost them dearly. They prefer to forego a powerful means of success, rather than run the accompanying risks. However they are less hesitant about joining political associations, which seem to them without risk because they do not involve money. They cannot participate very long before they learn how to maintain order among a large group of people, and the process that keeps them moving forward, harmoniously and methodically, toward a shared goal. They learn to submit their will to that of the others, to subordinate their individual efforts to the group effort, both things that are equally important in both voluntary and political associations.

The political associations can thus be considered as providing free education, schools in which all citizens learn the general theory of association.

Even though a political association does not directly help advance the cause of a civil one, destroying the former would damage the latter.

When citizens cannot form associations except in certain cases, they see an association as a singular and an uncommon process and they almost never think to use it.

When they are free to form associations in everything, people come to see associations as the universal, almost the only, means of reaching their diverse goals. Every new need awakens an idea for a new association. The art of association thus becomes, as I stated above, the founding science; everyone studies this science, and applies it.

When some associations are outlawed and others permitted, it is difficult to distinguish the former from the latter. In the confusion, all are avoided, and a kind of public perception is established that leads to a view that any association is something risky and almost illegal.

So it is misleading to think that the spirit of association, if it is suppressed in one aspect, will continue to develop as vigorously in all other aspects, and that simply allowing men to carry out a few endeavors jointly will lead them to do so enthusiastically. When citizens have both the ability and the habit of associating freely in everything, they will do so in small matters as well as large. But, if they are able to do so only in small matters, they will lose both the desire and ability. It will be useless to give them complete freedom to combine in business affairs: they will exercise only halfheartedly the rights they are granted; and, after the enormous amount of energy spent preventing the forbidden associations, it may come as a surprise to find that nothing will persuade them to undertake the permissible ones.

I am not saying that there cannot be civil associations in a country where political association is forbidden; men can never live together without undertaking some efforts in common. But I maintain that, in such a country, civil associations will always be very few, weak, and ineffectual, and they will never undertake great projects or will fail when they do so.

This leads me naturally to think that freedom of association in political matters is not nearly as dangerous to public tranquility as one thinks, and it may be that after a period of disturbing the state, it will actually strengthen it.

In democratic countries, one might say that political associations alone create the powerful individuals who aspire to govern. So governments today view these kinds of associations the same way kings in the Middle Ages viewed the powerful vassals of the crown: they feel a sort of instinctive horror toward them and fight them at every encounter.

However, they are favorable toward voluntary associations because they quickly realize that these do not necessarily lead people's thoughts to public affairs, and actually serve to distract them; by involving people more and more in projects that can only be achieved in peaceful times, voluntary associations are in fact turning them away from revolution. But they seem hardly aware that political associations actually increase and facilitate voluntary associations, and that by avoiding one threat they are depriving themselves of an effective remedy. When you see Americans engaged daily in free associations to advance a political point of view, promote a politician, or deny power to someone else, you may wonder how such independent people avoid falling into total licentiousness all the time.

When you consider, however, the infinite number of industrial enterprises that are pursued in common in the United States, and when you notice all around you Americans working tirelessly to achieve some important and difficult project, one that the slightest unrest would destroy, you easily see why such busy people are not at all inclined to disturb the government or destroy the public peace that is so beneficial to them.

Is it enough to see these things separately? Is it not necessary to discover the invisible knot that binds them? Americans from every state and of every point of view and of all ages acquire their shared preference for associations from the example of political associations, and it is there that they learn how to use them. That is where they come together, speak together, listen to one another, and join forces in all manner of projects. From these political associations they carry what they have learned back to civic life and apply them in a thousand ways.

Hence, by enjoying a dangerous level of freedom, Americans learn the art of minimizing the risks of freedom.

If one looks at a particular moment in the history of a nation, it is easy to say that political associations disturb the government and paralyze production; but if one looks at the whole life of a society, it is even easier to demonstrate that freedom of association in political matters is good for the prosperity and even the tranquility of all citizens.

In the beginning of this work I wrote: "Unlimited freedom of association should not be confused with freedom to write: the one is both less necessary and more dangerous than the other. A nation can apply any number of limits without losing its autonomy; at times it must do so in order to keep it." And later I added: "One cannot hide the fact that unlimited freedom of association in political affairs is, of all freedoms, the one that a society can least sustain. If such freedom does not actually lead to anarchy, it will come perilously close to doing so."

So I do not believe that it is always in a nation's best interest to allow absolute freedom of association in political affairs, and I even doubt the wisdom of unlimited freedom of association in any country, at any time.

It is said that no society can remain at peace internally, inspire respect for the law, or establish a permanent government without severely limiting the right of association. Those are all valuable qualities, to be sure, but I believe that, in order to attain them or keep them, a nation must accept from time to time certain strictures; but it is also necessary for it to recognize the costs.

I understand that one might amputate an arm to save his life, but don't tell me that a one-armed man will ever again be as adept as he was with two arms.

CHAPTER 21

Americans Overcome Individualism through the Doctrine of Self-Interest Well Understood

When the world was controlled by a small number of powerful and rich individuals, leaders held themselves to a lofty ideal regarding their responsibility: they liked to claim the virtue of selflessness and the godliness of altruism. For the time, that was the official doctrine in matters of morality.

I doubt that men were more virtuous in times of aristocratic rule than at other times, but people did speak constantly about the beauties of virtue; only in private did they consider how useful it might be. But, as aspirations were lowered and everyone thought about himself, moralists shied away from the idea of sacrifice and no longer dared

---

Chapter 21 appeared as Volume II, Part II, Chapter 8 in the original, complete text.

propose it to the human spirit; they settled for asking whether the individual citizen would benefit from working for the good of all, and whenever they saw one of those cases in which the individual good and the general good coincided, they were quick to point it out; in time, the number of such cases multiplied. What had been simply an isolated remark became a general doctrine and people came to believe that one helped oneself in helping others, that it was in one's own interest to do good works.

I have already shown several times in this work how the people of the United States have always known how to join self-interest with the general good. What I wish to point out here is the general theory that has brought them to this view.

In the United States, it is almost never said that virtue is beautiful. People defend it as useful, and prove it daily. American moralists never claim that one must sacrifice oneself for others because doing so is good; but they boldly affirm that sacrifices are just as necessary to the one who makes them as to those who benefit from them.

They have recognized that in this time and this country, an irresistible force requires each man to be self-reliant, and with no hope of halting this, they now think only of guiding him.

They no longer deny that man should follow his own self-interest, but they struggle to prove that it is in one's self-interest to be honest.

I certainly do not want to go into detail here about their reasoning, which would divert me from the subject; let it suffice to say that they have convinced their fellow citizens.

Long ago [Michel] Montaigne said, "If I do not choose the narrow path because it is narrow, I choose it because I have learned from experience that in the end it is usually the best and most useful path."

The doctrine of self-interest well understood is thus not a new one; but among the Americans today it has been universally adopted; it has been popularized and can be found as the basis for all activity; it is part of every speech. It is heard from the mouths of rich and poor alike.

In Europe, the doctrine of self-interest is much less refined than in America, but it is also less widespread and far less visible, and people continue every day to affect virtues they have lost.

Americans, by contrast, love to explain almost everything they do as self-interest well understood; they calmly explain how enlightened selfishness leads them to help each other and inclines them to sacrifice both time and money for the good of the State. I think that frequently they do not take enough credit for this; in the United States, as elsewhere, people often throw themselves naturally into a project without any thought for themselves; however, Americans rarely admit that they are doing so; they prefer to give credit to a philosophy than to themselves.

I could stop now and make no attempt to pass judgment on these words. My excuse would be the great complexity of the subject. But I do not want to use that excuse, and I would rather that readers, understanding my argument, disagree with me than to leave them in doubt about my meaning.

Self-interest well understood is not a lofty doctrine, but it is a clear and certain one. It does not claim to have great purpose; but it achieves those it sets effortlessly. Because it is within the intellectual reach of everyone, it is easily grasped and maintained. Accommodating itself remarkably well to human weakness, it readily attracts and holds a huge following, turning self-interest against itself both to harness and stimulate passions.

The doctrine of self-interest well understood does not produce passionate devotion; it encourages small sacrifices every day; by itself, it would not make a man virtuous; but it molds citizens who are disciplined, temperate, moderate, forward thinking, and self-directed; if it does not directly inspire a desire to be virtuous, it makes virtue almost second nature.

If this doctrine were to dominate morality entirely, examples of exceptional goodness might become rarer. I believe, however, that the most depraved behavior would be also be less common. The doctrine of self-interest well understood may prevent some men from rising very high above the norms of humanity; but there would be many more who would sink below them. It lowers the standard for individuals and raises it for mankind in general.

I would not hesitate to say that the doctrine of self-interest well understood seems to me, of all political theories, the one best adapted to the needs of people today, and I see in it the greatest protection they have from themselves. So the moralists of our day should turn to it first. Even when it is deemed imperfect, it should be adopted as essential.

In general, I do not believe we are more self-centered than Americans; the only difference is that there it is open and here it is not. Every American is able to make personal sacrifices to save others. We want to hold on to everything, and often we lose it all.

I see around me only people who seem to want to teach their contemporaries, by word and deed, that usefulness is never dishonest. Shall I not also find in that something that will make them understand that honesty can also be useful?

The spread of equality will inevitably lead to a greater quest for the useful, and there is no power on earth that can stop it or prevent every citizen from embracing it.

We can expect individual self-interest to become increasingly the primary, if not the sole, motivation for human activity; but it remains to be seen how each man will determine what is in his self-interest.

If, in becoming equal, the people remain ignorant and base, it is hard to imagine where the stupid excesses of their selfish interests will lead, nor how low they will sink in misery and shame if they are afraid to sacrifice some of their own well-being for the good of others.

I do not think the doctrine of self-interest, as it is preached in America, is evident in every respect; but it includes a great many truths so obvious that as soon as people are educated about them they are persuaded. So educate them, by all means: the century of blind devotion and instinctive virtue is long past, and I see a time coming when education will be essential to freedom, public harmony, and social order.

CHAPTER 22

The Taste for Material Comfort in America

In America the desire for material comfort is not always exclusive, but it is general; while it is not felt in the same way by everyone, it is a desire shared by everyone. The effort to satisfy the slightest physical needs and to provide anything to make life more convenient is a universal preoccupation.

The same thing is becoming increasingly apparent in Europe.

There are a number of reasons for this in both worlds that relate to my subject and I should point them out.

When wealth was inherited by the same families, we saw a large number of people living comfortably, but the desire for comfort was not their primary objective.

What most grips the human heart is not the satisfaction of owning valuable objects but the unfulfilled desire to own them and the constant fear of losing them.

Chapter 22 appeared as Volume II, Part II, Chapter 10 in the original, complete text.

In aristocratic societies, wealthy people have never known any other condition, and have no fear of it changing; rarely do they even imagine any other condition. Material comfort for them is not a reason for living; it is a way of living. For them it is a way of life to be enjoyed without reflection.

For them, the natural and instinctive desire that all men have to be comfortable is satisfied without effort or fear, and their minds are on other things; they aspire to higher things.

So members of an aristocracy will often evince a proud disdain for the comforts they enjoy so freely and a remarkable fortitude when they must finally give them up. Wherever revolutions have disrupted or destroyed aristocracies, we see how easily some people accustomed to great luxury are able to do without basic needs, whereas those who attained their comforts by hard work alone can hardly live once they are lost.

Moving from upper classes to lower ones, we find the same results, for different reasons.

Among nations dominated and immobilized by aristocracy, some people become used to poverty just as the rich grow accustomed to wealth. The latter are not preoccupied with their material well-being because it came to them without effort; the former give little thought to it because they have no hope of acquiring it and know too little of it to desire it.

In these societies the poor put their hopes on the next life; gripped by the miseries of everyday life, their spirits escape and seek joy beyond the day to day.

When, however, classes are mixed and privileges destroyed, when property is divided and education and freedom spread, poor people dream of a comfortable life, and the rich become afraid of losing it. The number of people of moderate means grows. They have enough to develop a real taste for material comforts and not enough to be satisfied with what they have. They will never have them without great effort and will give them up only with trepidation.

And so they strive constantly to acquire or retain these precious pleasures, which can neither satisfy nor endure.

The desire for material comfort is the best example I have found of a passion that is characteristic of men who are both motivated and limited by their obscure birth or limited resources. The desire for material well-being is essentially a middle-class one; it expands and increases with the expanding middle class; like it, the desire becomes preponderant. And from there it extends to both higher and lower social classes.

I have found no poor person in America who does not look with hope and envy at the comforts of the rich, or whose imagination does not aspire to advantages fate consistently withholds.

And I have found no one among the rich in the United States who has that fine disdain for material comfort that is sometimes observed among aristocrats in the most opulent and dissolute societies.

Most of these newly rich were poor once; they have felt the sharp pangs of poverty; they have struggled long against a harsh fate, and now that the battle is won, the old desires have survived; they are still drunk on the little pleasures they pursued for forty years.

As in every country, there are rich men in the United States with inherited wealth who enjoy an opulent lifestyle they did not have to work for. But even these few are no less attached to the pleasures of materialism. A love of comfort has become the dominant national feature; the whole flow of human passions is moving in that direction, and everyone is swept up in it.

CHAPTER 23

Why Americans Appear So Restless amid Their Prosperity

Occasionally, in some isolated provinces of the Old World, we find small groups of people who have been forgotten, so to speak, amid the universal tumult and who have remained untouched while everything around them has changed. Most of these people are uneducated and impoverished; they are not concerned with affairs of state and often they are oppressed. However, they appear generally serene and cheerful.

In America I have seen the freest, most educated and most prosperous people in the world; it seemed to me that their features were clouded; they looked serious and almost sad despite all their advantages.

The main reason for this is that the first group never thinks about the hardships it has, while the second never thinks of anything except the comforts it lacks.

Chapter 23 appeared as Volume II, Part II, Chapter 13 in the original, complete text.

It is a strange thing to see how feverishly the Americans pursue prosperity and how tormented they are all the time by a vague fear of having missed the fastest way of achieving it.

People in the United States cling to things of this world, as if they were immortal, and they make such haste to seize whatever is in reach, that one would think they are afraid of dying before they can enjoy the benefits. They grasp at everything but don't hold onto anything, dropping them to chase after new pleasures.

In the United States a man carefully builds a house in which to spend his old age, and he sells it before it is finished; he plants a garden, and boasts of it as if he were going to taste its fruits; he clears a field, and leaves it to others to reap the harvest. He embraces a profession and then gives it up. He settles in one place, but soon moves on, taking his fickle desires with him. When his personal affairs leave him some time, he enters the turmoil of politics. And when, near the end of a work-filled year, he has some free time remaining, his restless curiosity leads him to explore the vast territory of the United States. He will cover five hundred miles in a few days, the better to distract him from all his advantages.

Death finally overtakes and stops him before he has tired of this useless pursuit of a fulfilling happiness that stays always out of reach.

It is surprising at first to see this singular agitation that so many fortunate men evince, despite their affluence. It is a sight as old as the world; what is new is to see it in an entire population.

The love of material comforts must be recognized as the principal source of all this secret dissatisfaction that is revealed in the Americans' constant activity and in the capriciousness to be seen every day.

The person whose heart is closed to everything but a quest for worldly goods is always in a hurry, for he hasn't much time in which to acquire them, to possess and enjoy them. The knowledge that life is short goads him constantly. Quite apart from all that he has, he is always thinking about the thousands more that death will deny him, if he doesn't act quickly. This thought fills him with worry, fear, and regret, and now his soul is in a state of constant anxiety, making him always eager to change plans and move on.

If you add to this love of material prosperity a social condition in which laws and customs no longer force a man to remain in one place, he simply has one more thing to worry about; and so people are constantly changing direction, for fear of missing some shortcut to happiness.

In addition, it is clear that, while men who crave material comforts are passionate in their desires, they lose interest quickly; since pleasure

CHAPTER 23   WHY AMERICANS APPEAR SO RESTLESS

is the goal, the means of acquiring it must be quick and easy, for otherwise the trouble would surpass the pleasure. Most of these people are both passionate and weak, intense and anxious. Often death is less dreaded than the endless exertions leading to it.

Equality leads even more directly to several of the effects I have just described.

When all the privileges of birth and fortune are destroyed, when all professions are open to everyone, and when one can reach the peak of any of them on his own, a huge and comfortable career seems to open before men, and they are eager to see themselves called to greatness. But that view is mistaken and experience corrects it every day. The same equality that allows any citizen to conceive great dreams makes each one individually weak. It limits their power on every side, even as it allows their desires to grow.

Not only are they powerless by themselves, they encounter new and unimagined obstacles every step of the way.

The bothersome privileges of some have been destroyed; they compete with all. The standard has changed shape as well as position. When men are more or less alike, and follow the same path, it is difficult for any one of them to move quickly or break away from the solid crowd that surrounds and pushes them back.

The constant tension between the instinctive drive for equality and the limited means that it offers for achieving it torment and exhaust the spirit.

We might imagine that when men have reached a certain degree of freedom they would be completely satisfied. They would enjoy their independence without worry and without zeal. But men will never attain a satisfactory degree of equality.

Try as it might, a country will never be able to make men perfectly equal; and if, sadly, it ever did achieve absolute and complete leveling, there would still be inequality of minds that, coming from God, will always elude legislation.

No matter how democratic a society and a political constitution, it is certain that everyone will notice that he is surrounded by various controls and, stubbornly, these will be all he notices. When inequality is the law shared by everyone, the most striking inequities are hardly noticed; when everything is more or less on the same level, even the slightest are troublesome. That is why, as equality spreads, the desire for it becomes increasingly insatiable.

Among democratic nations, men easily obtain some equality; they can never have as much as they want. Perfection eludes them every day, but is never out of sight, and, men are drawn to the pursuit even as they see the goal recede. Men always think they are about to seize it and it always eludes their grasp. They see it clearly enough to recognize its appeal, but they never get close enough to enjoy it, and they die before having fully savored its pleasures.

These are the causes of that singular melancholia often noticed among people in democratic countries despite their prosperity, and also of the distaste for living that sometimes seizes them despite their comfortable and untroubled lives.

In France people complain that the suicide rate is growing; in America suicide is rare, but we are told that madness is more common than anywhere else.

These are different symptoms of the same illness.

Americans do not kill themselves, regardless of how miserable they may be, because religion forbids it and because materialist philosophy is virtually nonexistent for them, no matter how widespread their love of material prosperity.

So the will resists, but reason gives way.

In democracies, there are more pleasures than in aristocracies, and a far greater number of people enjoy them; however, one should remember that their hopes and desires are more frequently betrayed, their minds more troubled and anxious, their sorrows more bitter.

CHAPTER 24

How Americans' Love of Material Comfort Combines with the Love of Liberty and a Concern for Public Affairs

When a democratic state becomes an absolute monarchy, the activity that was formerly directed to both public and private affairs is abruptly concentrated on the latter, the result, at least for a while, is great material prosperity; the pace however soon slows, and productivity ceases.

I do not think one can find a single example of a manufacturing and commercial state, from Tyre to Florence to England, that was not free.

Chapter 24 appeared as Volume II, Part II, Chapter 14 in the original, complete text.

There is a direct connection and an essential one between these two: freedom and industry.

That is generally true of all nations, but especially of democratic ones.

I have already described how men who live during periods of equality have a constant need for association in order to acquire all the goods they desire, and, elsewhere, I showed how great political freedoms helped refine the art of association and put it in reach of everyone. Freedom, in such periods, is particularly useful for the production of wealth. It is clear, though, that despotism is especially hostile.

The nature of absolute power, in democratic times, is neither cruel nor brutal, but it is tedious and meddlesome. This kind of despotism, while it does not crush humanity underfoot, is directly opposed to the spirit of commerce and industry.

Men must be free, in democratic eras, in order to procure in freedom the material well-being they will always crave.

However, sometimes their excessive love of comfort causes them to accept the first leader they see. Then the love of prosperity turns against itself, and imperceptibly the object of all their desires moves further out of reach.

That is a real danger for those living in a democratic society.

When the love of material wealth grows faster than education and the lessons of liberty, some people become carried away seeing so many new things within their grasp. Thinking about nothing but making a fortune, they fail to see the direct connection between their own individual fortune and the prosperity of all. It isn't necessary to seize the rights such people possess; they give them up willingly. The exercise of political responsibilities seems to them an annoying waste of time, distracting them from their work. Electing representatives, mounting opposition to authority, or working as a community on communal business requires too much time; people don't have time to waste on useless projects. Those games are for people with time on their hands and not for busy men with more serious things to do. Those people believe that they are following the law of self-interest, but they have only the roughest idea about what that is, and so in order to attend to their own affairs, they neglect the most important thing, which is to remain masters of themselves.

Working people don't want to bother with public service and the class that might fill its leisure time by taking the responsibility no longer exists, so the role of governing is vacant, as it were.

If, in a time of crisis, an adept and ambitious person appears to seize power, he will find all the obstacles removed and any usurpation possible.

As long as he sees to it that the material interests of the people prosper, he will not have to answer for anything else. But above all he must keep the peace. Men who are passionate about material prosperity generally recognize the problems that social disorder creates for their prosperity before they understand how to use liberty to achieve it; and when any hint of public unrest invades the comfort of their private lives, they grow watchful and worried; the fear of anarchy holds them in constant suspense and they are always ready to suspend freedom at the first sign of disorder.

I readily agree that public peace is a great asset; but I do not want to forget that order can lead any people to tyranny. That does not mean that they should disregard public peace; but it must not be the only thing that matters. A nation that demands of its government nothing more than maintaining public order is already enslaved in its heart; it is the slave of its own prosperity, and the man who will put them in chains may come.

Despotism of factions is no less to be feared than the despotism of an individual.

When most people do not want to bother with anything but their personal affairs, even the smallest factions can dream of ruling over the public affairs.

So it is not unusual to see, both in the world at large as here at home, that a few people represent multitudes. These few alone speak in the name of the absent or distracted masses; they are acting alone in the midst of universal passivity. They decide, according to their own whims, everything; they change laws and tyrannize customs at will; it is surprising to see an entire population fall into the weak and unworthy hands of so few.

Until now, the Americans have happily avoided these perilous reefs just described; in that they are truly admirable.

There is perhaps no country on earth where one finds fewer lazy people than in America, and where everyone who works is fired up by the pursuit of prosperity. But if the Americans' love of material comfort is intense, at least it is not blind, and though reason cannot check the passions, at least it rules them.

An American is preoccupied with his own interests as if he were the only person in the world, and, a moment later, he takes up his public duties as if he has forgotten his own entirely. At one moment he seems motivated by selfish avarice, and the next by ardent patriotism. The heart of man cannot be divided like this. The People of the United States express alternately such a strong passion for both their prosperity and their liberty that we must believe these passions join somewhere deep in their souls and become one. In fact, Americans see that liberty is the best and greatest guarantee of their prosperity. They love these two things equally. They do not believe that involvement in public affairs is none of their business; on the contrary, they believe that their primary concern is to guarantee that government continue to allow them to obtain the goods they desire and that it never deprive them of enjoying in peace what they possess.

CHAPTER 25

How Aristocracy May Result from Industry

I have described how democracy favors the growth of industry and produces countless numbers of industrialists; we shall see the indirect path by which industry in turn may lead to the growth of an aristocracy.

We know that when a worker is not occupied with the same details every day, productivity increases more easily, rapidly, and economically.

We also know that the larger an industrial enterprise, the greater the capital investment, the cheaper products are to produce.

These facts have long been recognized, but we see clear evidence of them in our own time. We see them applied in many large industries, and increasingly in smaller ones.

I see nothing in the political world that should concern lawmakers more than these two new axioms of industrial science.

When a craftsman spends all his time on the fabrication of a single object, he acquires a singular skill in his work. However, he also loses the overall ability to concentrate his mind on the task. He becomes more skillful and less industrious every day, and we might say that as the work is perfected, the individual worker is degraded.

Chapter 25 appeared as Volume II, Part II, Chapter 20 in the original, complete text.

What can we expect from a person who has spent twenty years of his life making pinheads? And then what good is the powerful human intellect, that so often has moved the world, in such a person, except to find a better way to make pinheads!

When a workman spends a considerable part of his existence in this way, his mind thinks about nothing, day after day, except the object of his labor; his body acquires certain fixed postures from which he can no longer move. In short, he no longer belongs to himself but to the profession he has chosen. The fact that laws and customs have carefully broken down all barriers around him and opened a thousand different paths to prosperity is meaningless for him; an industrial theory more powerful than customs and laws has chained him to one occupation, and often to one place from which he is not free to leave. It has assigned him a particular position in society from which he cannot escape. Amidst universal motion, he is immobilized.

As the principle of the division of labor is applied more completely, the worker becomes weaker, more constrained, and more dependent. As the art advances, the artisan is forced backward. Additionally, as it becomes increasingly evident that industrial production becomes cheaper and better as manufacturing and investment grow, rich and wise men appear to exploit industries that previously were the domain of uneducated or poor artisans. They are drawn by the amount of effort required and the potential for enormous profit.

Consequently, as the science of industry is constantly degrading the status of the workers, it is advancing the status of people in power.

While the worker increasingly concentrates on a single detail, the view before the master is growing broader every day, and his mind expands as that of the worker shrinks. Soon the latter will need only physical strength without intellect; the former will need knowledge, almost genius, to succeed. The one increasingly comes to resemble the ruler of a vast kingdom and the other a wild animal.

The master and the laborer have nothing in common in this picture, and every day they grow apart. They are connected only as the links at the end of a long chain are connected. Each occupies the place made for him and never leaves it. One is in a state of constant, narrow, and essential dependence on the other, the one seemingly born to obey and the other to rule.

What, if not an aristocracy, is this?

As conditions of equality spread throughout a country, the market for manufactured objects expands; maintaining costs low enough to be within reach of people of modest means is the key to success.

As a result we see every day that the richest and shrewdest men devote their money and talent to industry and hope, by opening huge factories based on a strict division of labor, to satisfy the new demand apparent everywhere.

While the nation as a whole is turning to democracy, the industrial class becomes more aristocratic. Men begin to look more and more alike in the one, and more and more different in the other, and inequality grows in the society of the few as it decreases in the society as a whole.

Therefore, when we look back at the beginning, we seem to see the aristocracy emerging very naturally from the very core of democracy.

But this aristocracy is nothing like the one that preceded it.

First we see that, concerning itself only with industry and a handful of related professions, it is an exception, a freak, within the social context.

The small aristocratic societies created by certain industries within the great democracy of our day includes, like those of earlier times, a few who are very wealthy and a multitude in great poverty.

These poor people have few means of rising above their conditions and prospering, but the rich are constantly becoming poor, or leaving business without having realized any profit. Thus, the elements creating the poor classes are fixed, but the elements composing the rich are not. Actually, while there are many wealthy people, there is no wealthy class; for these individuals have no shared goals or values, traditions or background. There are many parts, but no whole.

Not only are the rich men not solidly united as a group, but we might say that there is really no link between the poor man and the rich man. They are permanently fixed next to each other; self-interest both unites and separates them simultaneously. The worker depends on the masters in general, but not anyone in particular. The two men see each other in the factory and nowhere else, and while they come together at one point, they remain far apart on every other. The manufacturer demands of the worker only his labor, and the worker expects nothing but a salary in return. The master is not responsible for protecting the worker, nor is the worker obliged to defend the master; and they are not permanently bound by either custom or duty.

The aristocracy based on business is almost never found living among the industrial population it manages; its interest is not in ruling the labor force, only in using it.

An aristocracy thus constituted will never have a firm hold on those it employs; and should it hold them momentarily, it will quickly lose them. It does not know what it wants and cannot act.

The landed aristocracy of the past was obliged by law, or believed itself obliged by custom, to come to the aid of its workers and to relieve their suffering. The manufacturing aristocracy today, having impoverished and brutalized those it uses, abandons them in a crisis to find food from a public charity. This is the natural result of all that preceded. There are frequent contacts between worker and master, but no real relationship.

I think that in general the manufacturing aristocracy we have seen emerge before our very eyes is one of the harshest that has ever appeared on earth; it is also one of the most limited and least dangerous.

It is to this, in sum, that the friends of democracy must turn a watchful eye; for if the permanent inequality of conditions and aristocracy ever should penetrate the new world, this is where they will enter.

Part III: Influence of Democracy on Customs as Such

CHAPTER 26

Education of Girls in the United States

There has never been a free society without morality and, as I said in the first part of this work, women create morality. Therefore, anything that contributes to the condition of women, their habits and opinions, seems to me to have great political significance.

In most protestant nations, girls are more responsible for their own actions than they are in Catholic ones.

This independence is even greater in protestant countries that, like England, have maintained or acquired the right of self-government. Freedom thus enters the family through political custom and through religious belief.

Chapter 26 appeared as Volume II, Part III, Chapter 9 in the original, complete text.

In the United States, Protestant doctrine combines with a very free constitution and very democratic social conditions; nowhere do young women enjoy freedom so early and so completely.

Long before a young woman reaches the age to marry, she is gradually freed from her mother's care; before she has entirely left her childhood, she thinks for herself, speaks freely, and acts alone; the whole world is spread out before her; far from trying to keep this hidden from her sight, she is shown more every day, and she is taught to see the world squarely and calmly. The vices and dangers of society are soon revealed; she sees them clearly, judges them without illusions, and faces them without fear; she is confident in her abilities, and her confidence seems to be shared by everyone around her.

One should almost never expect to find in young women in America the virginal naïveté and burgeoning desires, the innocent grace and guilelessness that in European girls is part of the passage from childhood to youth. It is rare for an American girl of any age to show timidity and childish ignorance. Like young girls in Europe, she wants to please, but she knows just how much it costs her. She may resist doing evil, but she knows what it is; rather than a chaste mind, she has pure morals. I have often been amazed and almost frightened by the singular ease and cheerful boldness with which these young American women navigate the reefs of witty conversation. A philosopher might stumble a hundred times on the narrow paths they traverse without accident or difficulty.

One quickly realizes that, even in childhood, when she has so much independence, the American girl never stops exercising self-control; she enjoys all the pleasures she is permitted without ever abandoning herself to any of them, and her reason never really drops the reins, even when she seems to let them flutter.

In France, where we still combine, in an odd way, the remnants of ages past in our opinions and tastes, we often provide women with a timid, withdrawn, and almost cloistered education, as they received in aristocratic times, and then we abandon them abruptly, without guidance or recourse, to the social chaos that is inseparable from democratic society.

Americans are more consistent.

They have learned that at the heart of democracy, individual independence must be great; youth is impatient, desires difficult to restrain; customs are always changing and public opinion often uncertain or helpless; paternal authority is weak and authority in marriage questioned.

Under these circumstances, they decided that there was little chance anyone could repress in women the most tyrannical desires of the heart, and that it would be safer to teach her to control them herself. As they were not able to protect her virtue from risk, they wanted her to know how to defend it herself, and they relied more upon the strength of her free will than upon barricades that could be overcome. Instead of holding her against her will, they constantly seek to increase her reliance upon her own strengths. Having neither the possibility nor the desire to keep girls in perpetual and complete ignorance, they hasten to teach her about things at an early age. Far from trying to conceal from her the corruptions of the world, they want her to see them first, and then struggle on her own to resist them, and they prefer to guarantee her virtue than to overvalue her innocence.

Although Americans are a very religious people, they have not depended upon religion alone to protect a woman's virtue; they have also sought to arm her reason. In this they have followed the same pattern as in other things. First they have gone to great lengths to make individuals responsible for their own freedom, and only then, when human strength is no longer sufficient, do they look to religion for help.

I realize that such an education is not without risk; I also know that it tends to develop judgment at the price of imagination, and to make women virtuous and cold, rather than tender and cordial companions for men. While society may be more peaceful and orderly, private life may hold fewer charms. But those are secondary ills and should be confronted for the good of all. Having come this far, we have no choice: a democratic education is essential to protect women from the dangers of the democratic institutions and mores that surround them.

CHAPTER 27

The Young Woman as Wife

In America, a woman's independence is permanently lost in marriage. If young women are less restrained there than anywhere else, as wives they submit to greater obligations. In her father's house, a girl

Chapter 27 appeared as Volume II, Part III, Chapter 10 in the original, complete text.

enjoys freedom and pleasure, whereas a wife lives in her husband's house as in a cloister.

These contrasting circumstances are perhaps not as contradictory as one would think, and it is natural that Americans should pass from one to the other.

Religious people and industrial nations have a particularly strict notion of marriage. Some see correct behavior in a wife as a sign of moral purity. Others believe that it assures domestic harmony and prosperity.

Americans are both a puritan nation and a commercial people; their religious beliefs and their industriousness have led them to demand of women self-abnegation and constant sacrifice of pleasure for work, something that is rarely asked of European women. As a result, in the United States the unavoidable pressure of public opinion confines a woman to a small round of domestic concerns and duties, and prevents her escaping them.

These firmly established attitudes are all around American girls from birth; she sees the rules that flow from them; she becomes quickly convinced that she could not stray for even a moment from contemporary customs without immediately risking peace of mind, honor, and her place in society; she finds the strength required to submit to the rules in the firmness of her mind and in the robust habits acquired through education.

One could say that in her independence she draws the courage to make the sacrifice without struggle or complaint when the time for that comes.

Moreover, an American woman does not fall into marriage as if into a trap, out of ignorance and simplemindedness. She has learned what is expected of her well in advance, and she assumes the burden of her own free will. She accepts her new position with courage, because she has chosen it.

Because paternal discipline is very lax and the conjugal tie very strict, a young woman enters a marriage cautiously and with circumspection. There are relatively few early marriages. American women marry only when their minds are experienced and mature; in other countries, most women do not typically begin to use and develop their minds until after marriage.

Furthermore, I am far from believing that the great transformation that occurs once a woman in America has married is due simply to the demands of public opinion. Often it is self-imposed through an act of will.

When the time comes to choose a husband, cold and austere reason, which free examination of the world has enlightened and strengthened, leads an American woman to consider lighthearted independence in marriage as a source not of pleasure but of perpetual woe; to see that the girlish amusements cannot become the recreation of a wife and that, for a married woman, the source of her happiness is in the marital home. Seeing clearly in advance, the only path that leads to domestic happiness, she takes it and from the first step proceeds without looking back.

The same strong will shown by young American wives in their immediate and uncomplaining assumption of the heavy burden of their new state, is also seen in the great trials they face throughout their lives.

In no other country in the world are private fortunes so precarious as in the United States. It is not unusual for one man to move up and down the ladder from poverty to wealth during his lifetime.

American women endure these upheavals calmly and with indomitable energy. Her desires seem to decline with her fortune as easily as they expand.

Most of the adventurers who go out to settle the western wilderness belong, as I said in my earlier book, to the old Anglo-American stock of the north. Many of these men who rush boldly off in search of wealth are people who were enjoying prosperity in their former situations. They take with them their wives, imposing on them the perils and poverty that are always endured at the beginning of such enterprises. I have often encountered on the edge of the frontier young women who, after being raised comfortably in the major towns of New England, have gone from the wealthy homes of their parents directly to an exposed cabin deep in the woods. Fever, loneliness, boredom have done nothing to break their courageous spirits. Their features are altered and faded, but their gaze is strong. They appear to be at once sad and resolute.

I have no doubt that these American women acquired the internal strength they needed from their early education.

In the United States, the girl she was can be seen in the wife she has become; her role has changed, her ways are different, but her spirit is the same.

How Social Equality Helps Maintain Moral Behavior in America

Some philosophers and historians have said, or suggested, that morality among women is more or less strict depending upon their distance from the equator. This is a poor excuse for an explanation; according to this, a globe and compass would explain one of the most difficult problems of humanity.

In my opinion, the facts do not support this materialistic theory.

At different times in history we find that the same country may be virtuous or dissolute. The conditions that regulate morality change over time; they do not simply reflect the nature of the country, which does not change.

I do not deny that in some countries the passions arising from sexual attraction are particularly intense; but I think that this natural intensity can always be stimulated or checked by social conditions and political institutions.

As different as the many visitors to America are in various ways, all agree that morality there is infinitely stricter than anywhere else.

It is clear that, on this point, Americans are better than their English forefathers. A superficial glance at the two nations offers sufficient evidence of this.

In England, as in every European country, women are publicly maligned for their weakness. Philosophers and politicians are often heard complaining about their lack of morality, and it is taken for granted in literature all the time.

In all American books, including novels, the chastity of women is accepted as certain, and there is no talk of romantic exploits.

The remarkable propriety of American morality is due, no doubt, partly to the country itself, partly to the Americans' ancestry, and partly to religion. But these causes are also found elsewhere and they are not sufficient as an explanation. The specific reason must be sought elsewhere.

I believe the reason lies in equality and the institutions that flow from it.

Chapter 28 appeared as Volume II, Part III, Chapter 11 in the original, complete text.

Conditions of equality alone do not produce uniformity of morals; yet there can be no doubt that it contributes to and strengthens morality.

Among aristocratic societies, birth and fortune often make men and women so different that it almost seems as if nothing can bring them together. Passion draws them, but social status and the notions that arise from that prevent them from uniting in a permanent and public way. The result is a large number of secret and momentary unions. Thus human nature compensates privately for the limits put on it by law.

This is not so when social equality has removed all imaginary or actual barriers that separated men and women. Every young woman believes she will become the wife of the man of her choice; this makes immoral behavior before marriage very difficult. There is no way a woman can tell herself that a man loves her, no matter how gullible passion may be, if he is free to marry her and fails to do so.

The same thing is true, though less directly, within marriage.

In the eyes of those involved and of those who are merely observers, nothing legitimizes an illicit love affair more than a forced or random marriage.

However, in a country where women are free to exercise their preference and where education has rendered them capable of choosing, public opinion is harsh toward her mistakes.

The severity of Americans is due partly to this. They consider marriage as a contract that is often onerous, but every clause of which must be strictly obeyed; the terms of the contract are well known in advance, and entered into freely, without coercion.

Fidelity becomes more obligatory and also easier.

In aristocratic countries marriage was meant to unite property rather than persons; sometimes the groom became engaged as a schoolboy and while his wife was still in the nursery. It is hardly surprising that the conjugal ties binding the fortunes of these two people left their hearts to stray. It was a natural consequence of the spirit of the contract.

When, however, everyone is free to choose his mate, without external interference or direction, it is usually only shared tastes and thoughts that bring a couple together; and this very similarity is what keeps them together.

Our fathers had developed a singular notion of marriage, actually.

Observing that the small number of marriages made as a love match in their day were almost always disastrous, they became firmly convinced that in such matters it was dangerous to be led by the heart. They thought chance could read the future better than choice.

Clearly, however, the examples they had before them proved nothing.

I will first point out that while women in democratic societies are given the freedom to choose a husband, their minds have first been opened through education and their wills strengthened enough to make such a choice; in aristocratic societies, however, young women secretly escape from parental authority in order to throw themselves into the arms of a man whom they have no time to come to know and no ability to judge, and so lack any such assurances. It is not surprising that they misuse their freedom the first time they exercise it; nor is it surprising that they make dismal mistakes when, without having the education available in a democratic society, they try to follow the customs of democracy.

That is not all.

When a man and a woman in an aristocratic society wish to marry despite their social inequality, they must overcome immense hurdles. After breaking or loosening the ties of filial obedience, they must ultimately escape the overwhelming force of custom and popular opinion as well; and when at last they reach the end of this brutal exercise, they find themselves outcasts among their friends and relations; the prejudice that they defied separates them. It is not long before their courage fails and their hearts grow bitter.

Consequently, when a couple in such a union is unhappy from the beginning and later unfaithful, we should not place the blame on freedom of choice but rather on the experience of living in a society that does not permit such choice.

Moreover, we should not forget that the same bold effort required of a man who challenges conventional errors almost always leads to irrational action; to dare to declare war on his own time and people, even when doing so is justified, requires a bold and an adventurous kind of mind, and people with this sort of character, whatever path they follow, rarely find happiness and virtue. And I might add in passing that this is why, in the most necessary and legitimate revolutions, one rarely finds moderate and impartial revolutionaries.

When, in an aristocratic era, an individual happens to decide to be guided in matters of marriage not by convention but only by his own desires, we should not be surprised to see the union lead rather quickly to immoral behavior and misery. However, there is no doubt that when this pattern of behavior is the natural and ordinary way of things and social conditions favor it, when there is paternal backing and public approval, then the internal harmony of families grows and marital fidelity is assured.

Most people in democracies are involved in politics or a profession, and at the same time modest financial circumstances require that women stay at home in order to manage personally and carefully the running of the household.

All these different jobs and obligations become natural barriers that, separating the sexes, mean the demands of the one are fewer and less vexing, and the authority of the other more lenient.

I do not mean that equality can itself make a man chaste, but it does reduce the menace of immoral behavior. Since no one now has the leisure or opportunity to threaten the virtue of women, we see that there are both many loose women and a multitude of honest women.

This state of affairs leads at times to regrettable personal unhappiness, but it does not depress and weaken the society at large; it does not damage family ties and weaken the country's morals. What does endanger society is the corruption of the few and the loose morals of all. To the lawmaker, prostitution is much less serious than philandering.

This tumultuous and constantly stressful life of men in democracies does more than just deny men the leisure time for love affairs; it actually removes the possibility in a way that is less obvious but more sure.

All men living in democratic times adopt to some extent the mental attitudes of the commercial and industrial classes; their minds are on more serious things, both calculating and positive; it turns less toward the ideal than toward some visible and tangible goal that he sees as the natural and necessary object of his desires. Equality does not destroy fantasy, but it limits it and keeps its flight close to the earth.

No one is less a dreamer than a citizen of democracy, and you almost never see anyone who wants to pursue idle and solitary thoughts that precede the ordinary and produce great emotions.

Americans do, it is true, put a high value on achieving that sort of deep affection, constant and peaceful, that gives life its sweetness and security; they do not pursue those turbulent and capricious emotions that trouble and shorten life.

I know that what I have written here applies fully only to America and does not apply, at the present time, in any widespread way to Europe.

In the half century during which laws and customs have, with unusual force, propelled several European countries toward democracy, we have not seen relations between the sexes become more controlled and more virtuous; in some places, in fact, we see the opposite. Certain classes are strict, but in general morality is looser. I say this without hesitation, for I no more aim to flatter my contemporaries than to condemn them.

This fact should trouble us, but not surprise us.

The beneficial influence that democracy can exercise on morality is one of those things that can appear only over a long time span. While social democracy favors good morals, the labor involved in creating conditions of equality does not.

CHAPTER 29

What Americans Mean by Equality of Men and Women

I have shown how democracy breaks down or modifies the different inequities that societies establish; but is that all, and doesn't it finally deal with the enormous inequality of men and women that has always seemed, right up to our own day, to be a fundamental law of nature?

I believe that the social movement that has brought to the same level fathers and sons, servants and masters, the inferior and the superior, also elevates the status of women and will make them increasingly the equal of men.

But in this especially I feel the need to make myself very clear; there is no subject about which the ignorant and confused thinking of this century has taken greater liberties.

There are some people in Europe who, confusing the different attributes of the sexes, claim that men and women are not just equal but alike. They give them the same roles, assign them the same duties, and grant them the same rights; they combine them in every area of work, pleasure, and business. It is easy to understand that by thus forcing the equalization of the sexes, both are degraded; and that so crudely mixing up the work of nature will result only in weakening men and corrupting women.

Chapter 29 appeared as Volume II, Part III, Chapter 12 in the original, complete text.

This is not the way the Americans have understood the kind of democratic equality that can be established between women and men. They thought that, since nature had created such a great difference between the physical and moral constitutions of men and women, its purpose was clearly to give their different abilities different tasks; and they felt that progress did not consist in making such different beings perform roughly the same tasks, but in allowing each to play his part as well as possible. Americans have applied to the two sexes current laws of political economy that govern industry. A careful division of labor between men and women ensures that the society's important work is done most effectively.

America is the one country in the world that has taken most care over time to lay out clearly separate paths for the two sexes and also to ensure that the two walk as equals but always on separate paths. You never see American women managing businesses outside the home, making contracts, or entering the political sphere; but neither do you see anyone forced to work as rough laborers or in demanding jobs that require physical strength. There are no exceptions, no matter how poor a family might be.

If American women are not able to leave their quiet domestic duties, neither are they ever required to do so.

So American women, who often reveal masculine reasoning and are as energetic as men, still maintain in general a very delicate aspect and are feminine in their manners, even though they sometimes seem like men in mind and heart.

Moreover, Americans never believed that democratic principles would result in upsetting marital relations or lead to confusion of authority in families. They believe that every association must have a leader and that the natural leader in marriage is the man. They do not, therefore, deny him the right to exercise authority over his partner; and they believe that, in the intimate world of a man and wife, as in the larger political world, the purpose of democracy is to regulate and give legitimacy to the necessary power, not to destroy all power.

This attitude is not held solely by one sex and opposed by the other.

I have not found that American women consider conjugal authority as a fortuitous usurpation of their rights, nor that they believe that they are degraded or made subordinate by it. I think, though, that they have made something glorious of this voluntary yielding of will, and that they feel worthier for bending to the yoke rather than trying to avoid it. That at least, is the sentiment expressed by the most virtuous of them; others are quiet about it, and one never hears an adulterous spouse loudly proclaiming the rights of women, while trampling on her most sacred duties.

In Europe people often remark on a degree of contempt detectable in the flattery that men lavish on women: although a European man is often a woman's willing slave, it is obvious that he never actually considers her an equal.

In the United States, one rarely praises women; but she is always accorded respect.

Americans constantly reveal their total confidence in the good sense of a spouse and a deep respect for her freedom. They consider her mind the equal of a man's at uncovering the bare truth and her heart just as firm in facing it; they have never thought to shelter the virtue of one more than in prejudice, ignorance, or fear.

It seems that in Europe, where men readily submit to the tyrannical influence of women, they nevertheless deny them the most basic privileges of the human race and consider them to be seductive and imperfect; and it should not surprise us that women come to see themselves in the same way, and they almost feel it a privilege to be helpless, weak, and frightened. This is not a right that American women are demanding.

Moreover, one could say that in matters of morals, we have given men a sort of singular immunity; it is as if there is one kind of virtue for him and another for his partner; and, according to public opinion, the same behavior may be either a crime or simply a mistake.

Americans do not recognize this unequal division of rights and responsibilities. For them, the seducer is just as dishonored as his victim.

It is true that Americans rarely show those thoughtful attentions that women in Europe receive from every quarter; but in their daily behavior they attest to her virtue and delicacy, and they have such a high regard for women's moral freedom that in the presence of women everyone carefully watches his language for fear that they might say something to offend. In America, a young woman is able to set out, alone and unafraid, on a long journey.

Lawmakers in the United States, who have softened almost all of the regulations in the penal code, punish rape with death; and there is no crime that public opinion pursues with greater zeal. It is simple: as Americans feel that nothing is more precious than a woman's honor, and nothing so deserving of respect as her independence, they feel that no punishment is too harsh for those who would rob her of it.

In France, where the same crime is treated much more gently, it is often hard to find a jury to convict. Is this contempt for prudishness, or contempt for women? I have to believe it is both.

Thus, Americans do not believe that a man and a woman have either the right or responsibility to do the same things, but they show an equal respect for the roles of each, and they consider them to be persons of equal worth but destined for different things. They certainly do not think a woman's courage looks the same as that of a man, or useful for the same things; but they do not deny that she is courageous; and while they do not believe that a man and his wife must use their minds and their intellects in the same way, they at least believe that they are equally rational and their minds equally clear.

By allowing the inferiority of women to endure in society, Americans have worked mightily to elevate her intellectually and morally to the level of men; in this I believe they have admirably grasped the true meaning of democratic progress.

Speaking for myself, I can say without hesitation: although women in the United States almost never leave their homes, and are, in some respects, quite dependent there, I believe her status is higher there than anywhere else; if, as I approach the end of this book in which I have tried to describe so many American achievements, I were asked to give the most important reason for the singular prosperity and growing power of the Americans, I would say that it is the superior status of American women.

CHAPTER 30

American Society Appears Both Restless and Monotonous

There is almost nothing so apt to arouse and sustain curiosity than the appearance of the United States. Fortunes, ideas, and laws are changing constantly. One could say that immutable nature herself is changing, so altered is it every day by the hand of man.

Chapter 30 appeared as Volume II, Part III, Chapter 17 in the original, complete text.

However, in the end this constant flux appears monotonous, and after having observed this moving panorama, the viewer grows bored.

In aristocratic society, everyone is more or less fixed in one social sphere, but within that sphere people differ widely; they have different passions, ideas, habits, and tastes. Nothing changes, yet everything is different.

In democracies, however, all men are alike and do more or less the same things. They are subject, it is true, to great and constant tribulations; however, since the same successes and failures recur over and over again, the plot is always the same and only the names of the actors change. American society looks busy, because the people and events are constantly changing; it is monotonous, because all those changes are the same.

Men living in democratic times have many passions, but their passions lead mainly to a love of money or are the product of it. It is not that their souls are smaller, but that the importance of money is so great.

When all citizens are independent and indifferent, their support can only be had at a price, which multiplies *ad infinitum* the purposes of wealth and raises the value of it.

The prestige that once attached to the old ways has disappeared, and men are no longer, or are only slightly, distinguished by birth, station, and profession; only money is left as a highly visible indication of the differences between them and it alone is capable of raising some above the rest. Distinctions based on wealth increase as all others decline and disappear.

Among aristocrats, money leads to only a few points on the vast ring of desires; for people in democracies, it seems to lead to all of them.

Again we find that an American's love of money is either the primary or secondary basis for everything he does; this means that all passions look very familiar, and the picture grows quickly tiresome.

This constant repetition of the same passions is monotonous; as are the particular means of satisfying them.

In a stable and constitutional democracy like the United States where one cannot grow rich through war, public office, or political spoils, the love of money steers a man into industry. But industry, which so often leads to great unrest and great failure, cannot prosper except by very consistent habits and a long succession of uniform, small tasks. The greater the ambition, the more consistent the habits and uniform the acts. It is the very intensity of their desires that causes Americans to act methodically. Ambition may trouble their minds, but it orders their lives.

What I am saying here about Americans is true of almost all people today. Diversity is disappearing from the human race; the same ways of acting, thinking, and feeling are found in all corners of the world. That is not simply because people are conforming and emulating each other more, but because in every country people are moving farther away from the ideas and attitudes of a particular cast, profession, or family and are coming almost simultaneously to a broader view of human nature that is universal. Although they are not imitating each other, they are becoming more alike. They are like travelers spread across a huge forest whose paths are all leading to the same point. If all of them perceive the central point at the same time and turn their steps toward it, they will imperceptibly come closer together and, in the end, without trying, without even seeing or recognizing each other, they will be surprised to find themselves all at the same place. All people who aim to study and emulate not any one individual but mankind as a whole will ultimately come together around shared social mores just as travelers meet at a central point.

CHAPTER 31

Why Great Revolutions Will Become Rare

[. . .]

Although Americans are constantly changing or repealing various laws, they are far from exhibiting any revolutionary fervor. From the speed with which they check themselves and calm down whenever public unrest becomes a threat, at the very moment when passions run highest, it is clear that they abhor revolution as the worst of all evils and everyone resolves inwardly to make any sacrifice to avoid one. There is no country in the world where feelings about property are stronger, or cause greater anxiety, than in the United States, or where the majority are less favorable to doctrines that challenge in any way whatsoever the distribution of wealth.

Chapter 31 appeared as Volume II, Part III, Chapter 21 in the original, complete text.

I have often noticed that theories that are revolutionary by nature, and that could only be realized by a complete and sometimes abrupt change in the distribution of private property, find far less favor in the United States than in the great monarchies of Europe. While some may profess such theories, most people instinctively reject them in horror.

I dare say that most of the slogans normally considered democratic in France would be forbidden in the democracy of the United States. The reasons are clear. In America, ideals and passions are democratic; in Europe we still harbor ideals and passions that are revolutionary.

If America ever does experience great revolutions, they will be the result of the presence of blacks living on American soil; in other words, caused not by equality of conditions, but rather by their inequality.

When conditions are equal, people are content to live apart from each other, and ignore the crowd. Legislators in democratic countries must be careful to correct this tendency, rather than encourage it in the belief that it will help to steer citizens away from political passions and thus be a deterrent to revolutions: otherwise, they might in the end actually bring about the very evil they are trying to avoid, and the time could come when the unchecked passions of the few, supported by the ignorant egoism and cowardice of the majority, would subject the body politic to bizarre social changes.

In democratic societies there are only a few small minorities who desire revolution; but minorities are sometimes able to produce it.

I am not saying that democratic societies are safe from revolution, simply that the social conditions of these countries do not draw them to it, and in fact lead away from revolution. Democratic countries, when left alone, do not naturally engage in great causes; they are brought to revolutions only against their will, and while they must sometimes experience one, they do not start them. And I would add that, when such people have been given the chance to acquire education and experience, they prevent them.

I know very well that public institutions themselves have a lot to do with these matters; they can encourage or oppose the instincts that grow out of social conditions. I repeat, I am not claiming that countries are protected against revolution simply by virtue of conditions of equality; but I do believe that whatever institutions such people might have, major revolutions will always be infinitely less violent and more rare among them than one might suppose; and I easily imagine a political state that, in partnership with equality, will build a more stable society than has ever been seen in our western world.

Some of what I have just said about actions also applies in part to ideas.

There are two very surprising things about the United States: the great variation in almost all human activity and the singular permanence of certain principles. People are moving constantly, yet their minds seem almost incapable of change.

Once an idea takes root and spreads across the land, no power on earth can remove it. In the United States general doctrines in matters concerning religion, philosophy, morality, and even politics vary almost not at all, or at least they are modified only after almost imperceptible and covert effort; even the most blatant prejudices disappear only after a very long time, given the constant to and fro of men and things.

I hear people say that it is in the nature and customs of democracies to change feelings and ideas all the time. That may be true in small democratic countries, such as those of antiquity, in which everyone gathered in a public place and then responded to the call of an orator. I have seen nothing comparable with the great democratic country that exists on the other side of the ocean. What has struck me in the United States is the difficulty one has to correct some idea held by the majority and then to separate the majority from a leader it has embraced. Nothing you could write or say would succeed; that can happen only with experience. Sometimes even experience must repeat itself.

If this is at first surprising, a closer look explains it.

I do not think it is as easy as one might think to remove prejudices from democratic countries; to change beliefs; to substitute new religious, philosophical, political, or moral principles for those that have become entrenched; in short, to effect serious and frequent intellectual revolutions. It is not that the human mind is lazy; it works all the time; but it works harder to multiply the variations of consequences of known principles and to discover new consequences than to search for new principles. It is better at going around in circles than at moving quickly and directly forward; it slowly expands its sphere with constant hasty, small actions; it does not move all at once.

Men who are equal in rights, education, fortune, and condition generally will necessarily differ very little in their needs, habits, and tastes. Because they view things from the same perspective, their minds too are naturally drawn to think alike, and while each of them is free to part company with his contemporaries and think for himself, in the end they come back together, without meaning or intending to, to certain shared opinions.

The more I observe closely the effects of equality on intellect, the more I am persuaded that the intellectual anarchy we have seen is not, as many suppose, natural to democratic countries. I believe that should rather be viewed as a particular accident of their youth, and that it appears only during that stage in the process when men have already broken the bonds that once held them together, and yet their origins, education, and customs are very different; and then, having held onto these different ideas, instincts, and tastes, there is nothing to impede their acting on them. The opinions of most importance to people become alike to the extent that conditions are alike. That seems to me to be a general and enduring fact; the rest is random and transitory.

I believe that, on rare occasions, individuals will emerge within a democracy who conceive, suddenly, a system of thought that is far from the one adopted by his contemporaries; when such an innovator appears, I imagine that he will have great difficulty being heard, and even more making himself believed.

When conditions are almost equal people are not easily persuaded by others. Since they see each other at close range, learn together the same lessons, and lead similar lives, they are not inclined to accept one of their own as a leader to be followed blindly: people rarely trust the opinions of those like themselves.

It is not simply that confidence in the wisdom of a particular individual is weakened in democratic societies, but, as I have said before, the very notion of the intellectual superiority of anyone over others is one that fades quickly.

As people become more alike, the dogma of intellectual equality slowly takes hold and it becomes difficult for any innovator, whoever he may be, to gain and exercise much influence over the minds of a people. In such societies, abrupt revolutions are rare, and if we look at the history of the world we see that sweeping changes in popular opinion are produced less by strength of argument than by the authority of a single name.

Furthermore, remember that in democratic societies people are not bound by formal ties to each other; they must be persuaded to cooperate. In aristocratic society, however, the power to persuade a few is enough; others will follow. If Luther had lived in a period of equality, and not been heard by lords and princes alone, he would have had much more difficulty changing the face of Europe.

It is not because men living in a democracy are naturally convinced of the certainty of their own opinions that they are so firm in their views; they often have doubts that no one, in their opinion, can resolve. At such times it seems that the human mind would readily change position, but as nothing is either pressuring or steering it, it vacillates and does not budge.

When one has gained the confidence of a democratic country, it still takes a major effort to hold its attention. It is very difficult to be heard by people living in democracies, unless they themselves are the topic. They do not listen to what anyone says because they are always so preoccupied with what they themselves are doing.

One meets very few idle people in democratic nations. Life is spent in the midst of activity and noise, and people there are so busy acting that there is very little time left for thinking. What I wish to show, above all, is not only that they are busy, but that they are passionate about their work. They are constantly at work and their efforts are all-consuming; the heat created from the energy they expend at work prevents them from burning with ideas.

I believe that in a democracy it is very difficult to excite enthusiasm for any theory that does not have a visible, direct, and immediate relevance to daily living. Such people do not easily give up their old beliefs. It takes enthusiasm to propel the mind out of its well-worn grooves, and to make great intellectual revolutions as well as great political revolutions.

People living in a democracy have neither the time nor the inclination to go looking for new ideas. Even when they do begin to doubt the ones they have, they retain them because it would take too much time and study to change; they cling to them not out of certainty but out of familiarity.

There are still other reasons, and stronger ones, that impede straightforward shifts in attitudes in democratic countries. I presented them at the beginning of the book.

Just as the influence of individuals is weak and almost absent for people in democracies, the power exercised by the majority on the individual's thinking is enormous. The reasons for this are given elsewhere. What I want to say here is that it would be wrong to think that the form of government alone accounts for this, and that for the majority to lose its grip on opinion it would have to lose its political power.

In an aristocracy, men usually have their own status and power. When they find themselves out of step with a majority of their peers, they withdraw and find support and consolation within themselves. This is not at all true of democracies. There, public opinion seems as necessary to them as the air they breathe, and it is a kind of death to be out of favor with the majority. The latter has no need of laws to force the compliance of those who disagree with it. Disapproval is enough. The feeling of isolation and impotence overwhelms and grieves them.

Whenever conditions are equal, conventional opinion weighs heavily on every individual; it surrounds him, guides and oppresses him; that comes from the very makeup of society rather than from its laws. As men come to be more and more alike, each one feels weaker and weaker vis à vis others. Finding nothing that elevates him or distinguishes him from others, he mistrusts himself when confronted; not only does he lack the strength, but he begins to doubt himself, and he is close to acknowledging the error of his ways when the majority demands it. The majority does not need force; it persuades.

However one organizes and balances the powers of democratic society, it will always be very difficult to believe something rejected by the majority and to espouse a view it condemns.

This is a powerful spur to stability.

When an opinion has taken hold in a democratic society and is firmly fixed in the minds of the majority, it sustains and perpetuates itself effortlessly because no one challenges it. Those who first rejected it as false end up by taking it as fact, and those who continue to fight it in their hearts do nothing to reveal their feelings; they are careful to do nothing that would lead to a dangerous and useless conflict.

It is true that, when the majority in a democracy changes its mind about something, it can bring about unusual and abrupt reversals of opinion; but it is very difficult for it to change and it is almost imperceptible when it does.

It sometimes happens that time, events, or the efforts of a single intelligent person can slowly weaken or defeat a belief and leave not a trace of having done so. No one ever challenges these ideas publicly. There are no meetings to organize a fight. Former partisans slowly and silently fall away, and every day a few more people withdraw until only a handful maintain the old point of view.

It is still that way in this country.

As its enemies remain silent, or communicate their thoughts only furtively, they themselves are hardly aware that a great revolution has occurred, and, in their doubt, they remain silent. They watch and are silent. The majority no longer believes; but it pretends to believe, and this useless phantom of public opinion is enough to freeze out innovators and hold them in respectful silence. We are living in an age that has seen the most abrupt alterations in the minds of men. However, it may be that human attitudes will be more stable than they have been in any of the preceding centuries in history; this time has not yet come, but it may be near.

From my close study of the natural needs and instincts of democratic societies, I am convinced that, if ever equality should be established in a permanent and general way in the world, great intellectual and political revolutions will become most difficult, and rarer than anyone might suppose.

Since men in democracies seem to be constantly moved, uncertain, breathless, ready to change ideas and places, we think that they are suddenly going to abolish their laws. We forget that, if equality brings about certain changes, it also reminds men of the value of stability in attaining their goals; it prods them, and also checks them, propels them forward and keeps their feet on the ground, it inflames their desires and limits their power.

All of this is not obvious at first: the passions that separate citizens from each other in a democracy are self-evident. But less perceptible is the hidden force that anchors them and unites them.

Dare I say, in the midst of the ruins all around me, that what I fear most for the generations to come is not more revolutions?

If citizens continue to shut themselves off ever more tightly within the circle of their private interests, restless and discontented, it is foreseeable that they will close themselves off from the great and powerful public emotions that disturb people, but that develop and renew them. When I see property become entrenched, and the anxious and excessive love of property, I cannot help fearing that people will reach the point where they consider every new theory as a threat, every innovation as a nuisance, all social progress as a step toward revolution, and that they will completely resist any change for fear that it will sweep them away. I confess that I tremble at the prospect that they will become so beholden to their cowardly love of the pleasure they have that their concern for their own future and that of their grandchildren will disappear, and that they will prefer to follow sheepishly the course of destiny than to do anything sudden or extreme to change it.

We think that new societies are going to continue changing before our eyes every day, and yet I am afraid that they will ultimately be so entrenched in their institutions, prejudices, and customs that mankind will become stifled and narrow-minded; that the spirit will constantly reshape itself without producing new ideas; that human beings will wear themselves out in petty and, ultimately, useless personal activities; and that, despite being in constant flux, humanity will not progress.

Part IV: The Influence of Democratic Ideas and Attitudes on Politics

I would not fully realize my objective in writing this book if, after having shown the ideas and attitudes associated with equality, I did not indicate, in conclusion, the general influence these ideas and attitudes may have on government in human societies.

To do this, I will frequently have to retrace my steps. However, I hope the reader will not abandon me when familiar paths lead to a new insight.

CHAPTER 32

Equality Naturally Leads to a Desire for Free Institutions

Living in conditions of equality makes men more independent of one another and accustomed to doing exactly as they like in their personal affairs. Enjoying complete independence in relation to their peers and in the conduct of their private lives leads men to a suspicion of all authority and inspires ideas of political freedom. People living in such a time move naturally along a path that slopes toward free institutions. Take any one of them and try to discover his fundamental beliefs, if that is possible: you will find that, of all kinds of government, the one he thinks of first and values most is the one in which he elects the leader and controls the activities.

Of all the political effects produced by equality of conditions, this love of independence is the first thing one notices, and is what timid

---

Chapter 32 appeared as Volume II, Part IV, Chapter 1 in the original, complete text.

minds fear most; this fear is not unreasonable, for anarchy looks more frightening in democratic countries than anywhere else. Since citizens have little influence over each other, it seems that without the national government holding them all together, there would soon be chaos, with every citizen going his separate way, and society quickly reduced to dust.

Nevertheless, I am convinced that anarchy is not the greatest threat in democratic times but the least.

Equality actually results in two trends: one leads men directly to independence and can lead abruptly to anarchy; the other leads them by a longer, hidden, and more certain route to servitude.

People easily see the danger of the first and resist it; they let themselves be led along the other without even noticing it: it is especially important that they be warned.

Personally, far from blaming equality for the disobedience it inspires, that is the quality I most admire. I see it as the basis, in the heart and soul of everyone, of that vague notion of and instinctive penchant for political independence, and thus as offering the remedy for the very danger it creates. This aspect of equality appeals to me greatly.

CHAPTER 33

The Type of Despotism
Democratic Nations Have to Fear

During my stay in the United States I observed that democratic societies like that found in America are singularly vulnerable to the rise of despotism, and on my return to Europe I observed the extent to which most of our leaders have already adopted the ideas, sentiments, and needs created by that social order, in order to widen the circle of their power.

That has led me to believe that Christian nations may ultimately be subject to the kind of oppression comparable to that which many peoples in antiquity suffered.

Chapter 33 appeared as Volume II, Part IV, Chapter 6 in the original, complete text.

A more detailed examination of the subject and five years of new reflections have done nothing to remove my fears but have altered their focus.

At no time in the past was there ever a ruler so absolute and powerful that he attempted to administer alone, without the support of secondary authorities, every part of a great empire; never was there one who expected to subject all people without distinction to every detail of a uniform legal code, or who stooped to the level of the people to guide and govern their individual lives. The idea of such an undertaking never occurred to anyone and if it had, lack of education, imperfect administrative processes, and especially natural obstacles created by conditions of inequality would quickly have presented themselves to block the execution of such a grandiose plan.

We know that during the period when the Caesars were most powerful, the various people of the Roman world retained their diverse customs and morals; although all had to obey the same monarch, most of the provinces were administered separately; they contained powerful and vibrant cities, and although all governmental power in the Empire was concentrated in the hands of the emperor, and although ultimately he acted as the arbiter of all conflicts, the details of daily life in society and of individual existence were usually handled outside of his control.

It is true that the emperors wielded immense and absolute power, which allowed them free rein to employ all the power of the state to satisfy even the most outrageous ventures; they often abused their power to seize property or take lives arbitrarily: the brunt of their tyrannical power fell heavily on certain citizens; however, it did not reach the lives of most people; it was concerned with certain major undertakings and neglected the rest; it was brutal, and limited.

If despotism were to take hold in the democratic nations of our day, it would have a very different character: it would be milder but more far reaching, and it would not torment men but degrade them.

I have no doubt that in our own time of enlightenment and equality, rulers would more easily achieve control of all public authority and penetrate more regularly and more deeply into the private sphere than was ever possible for rulers of antiquity. However, equality both facilitates despotism and tempers it; we have shown how, as men become more alike and more equal, public morals become more humane and gentler; when there are no citizens with great power or wealth, tyranny lacks the opportunity and a stage. As all fortunes are modest, all passions are naturally restrained, imaginations limited, pleasures simple.

This universal moderation extends to the ruler himself and holds his desires within certain limits.

Apart from these reasons rooted in the very nature of social conditions, I could add many others that are outside my subject; I wish however to stay within the parameters I defined at the start.

Democratic governments may become violent and cruel in times of great turmoil and peril; but these crises will be rare and temporary.

When I think about the petty desires of people today, of their weak morals, the extent of their learning, the purity of religion, their lenient morality, their orderly industrious lives, I am less worried that leaders will become tyrants, and more worried that they will become guardians.

So I think that the kind of oppression that threatens democratic societies resembles nothing that has ever been seen before in the world; our contemporaries will have no memory of their type. Even I look in vain for an expression that can capture and reproduce what I see; the old words despotism and tyranny are inadequate. It is something new, and since I am unable to name it, I must try to define it.

I want to imagine the new face that despotism might have in the world: I see a mob of people, all alike and equal, perpetually going around in circles in pursuit of the petty, common pleasures to satisfy their souls. Each of them, standing alone, is a stranger to the destiny of the others; for each of them his own children and friends comprise the whole human race; each lives with his fellow citizens but doesn't see them; he touches them and feels nothing; he exists in himself and for himself alone, and though he may retain his family, one would have to say that he has lost his country.

Above them all stands a powerful schoolmaster, whose whole responsibility is to guarantee their pleasure and to watch over them. He is absolute, conscientious, methodical, all-knowing, and kind. He would resemble an all-powerful father figure if he were actually preparing his people for their coming of age; in fact, however, his goal is to keep them in perpetual infancy; he wants his citizens to enjoy themselves, as long as pleasure is all they think about. He will work hard on their behalf; but he wants to act alone, the ultimate arbiter; he will keep them safe, provide for their needs and ensure their comfort, conduct all business and direct all work, manage their inheritances, divide their property; why not remove the need for them to think at all, or deal with any of life's problems?

This is how independent decision-making withers; freedom to act is circumscribed until little by little citizens have been robbed of all autonomy. Equality prepares men for all these events; it disposes them to submit, and even to view them as beneficial.

Having finally placed every individual under his control, shaping the individual to his will, the all-powerful ruler wraps his arms around the entire society; he covers it with a network of complex little rules, uniform and petty, from which even the most original minds and hearty souls cannot see their way clear; the ruler does not break their will, but he weakens it, molds it and guides it; he rarely forces anyone to act, but he constantly opposes anyone taking action; he destroys nothing, he stifles everything; he does not tyrannize, but he annoys, compromises, saps, extinguishes, and numbs until finally he creates a nation of sheep, timid and hardworking, whose shepherd is the government.

I have always thought that the well-managed, subtle, and peaceful servitude I have just described could coexist with certain superficial freedoms better than anyone would expect, and that it is very likely to appear in the shadow of popular sovereignty.

Our contemporaries are constantly subjected to two conflicting passions: they feel the need to be led and the desire to remain free. Since they are unable to rid themselves of either of these desires, they try to satisfy them both. They imagine a single power, a guardian, all-powerful, but elected by citizens. They combine centralization with sovereignty of the people. That provides some relief and consoles them with the thought that while they are subordinate, they have at least chosen their guardians. All citizens agree to be tethered because they see that it is not an individual or a class that holds their chains but the people themselves.

In such a system, citizens momentarily step outside their dependency to choose a master only to surrender their autonomy again immediately afterward.

There are, today, many people who have no difficulty accommodating themselves to this type of compromise between administrative despotism and popular sovereignty, and who think that they have assured individual freedom, when they have actually delivered it to the national authority. This is not good enough for me. The nature of the master matters less than the surrender of autonomy.

Still, I do not deny that a constitution of that type is infinitely preferable to one in which all power is concentrated and bestowed upon an irresponsible individual or body. Of all the different forms that democratic despotism could take, the latter would surely be the worst.

When the ruler is elected or closely monitored by a truly elective and independent legislature, his power to oppress the individual is slightly greater; but it is always less degrading because any citizen who feels powerless and restricted is aware that in obeying he is submitting only to himself and that by giving up certain advantages he gains others.

I also understand very well that, when the ruler represents the country and depends upon it, the powers and rights that are taken away from the people do not serve the chief of state only but benefit the state itself and that individuals draw some benefit from sacrificing personal freedom for the public good.

To establish national representation in a highly centralized government helps to mitigate the evil that excessive centralization can cause, but it does not eliminate it.

I am well aware that individual participation in important matters is preserved in this way; but it is restricted nonetheless in small matters. It is often forgotten that the greatest danger lies in the small ways people are controlled. Personally, if I thought one could be sure of having one without the other, I would say that freedom in big things is less important than in small ones.

Subjugation in small things happens every day and is felt only vaguely by citizens. It does not cause them to despair; but it grates on them constantly and it makes them renounce free will. Over time it stifles the spirit and weakens the soul, while obedience, which is required only rarely and in a small number of critical areas, does not look like servitude except from afar, and weighs on relatively few people. It is in vain that the same citizens who have become so dependent on the central authority are called upon on occasion to choose the representatives of this power; this important exercise of the freedom to choose is too brief and too rare to prevent the erosion of the ability to think, to feel, and to act for themselves, and gradually the people decline to a state less than human.

Moreover, they soon become incapable of exercising the important and unique privilege that remains. The democratic people who introduced liberty into the political sphere, even as they allowed the spread of despotism in the administrative sphere, have seen fit to do some singularly strange things. They consider citizens incapable of dealing with minor issues in which the slightest common sense would suffice, whereas they grant them immense prerogatives in matters important for the whole country; citizens become either puppets of the ruler or its masters, more than kings and less than men. After examining all the different systems of election, and finding none that suits them, they are shocked and keep looking; as if the problems they found had more to do with the constitution of the country than with the electorate itself.

It is actually hard to imagine how men who have utterly renounced the habit of governing themselves could choose carefully those who are responsible for leading them, and no one would ever expect a liberal, energetic, and wise government to emerge from a subjugated people.

A constitution republican in its head and ultra-monarchical in all other parts, has always seemed to me a monstrous apparition. The vices of governors and the stupidity of the governed will quickly lead to disaster; and the people, weary of both leaders and themselves, will create freer institutions, or quickly revert to lying at the feet of a single master.

CHAPTER 34

An Overview of the Subject

Before leaving behind my research into the subject, I wish to cast one last look over all the different features of the face of the New World, and to judge the general influence that equality will ultimately have on men's futures; but the difficulty of such an undertaking holds me back; in the presence of such a large object, I feel my sight blurring and my mind reeling.

The new society that I have tried to portray and wished to evaluate is in its infancy. It is still being shaped by time; the great revolution it created is ongoing, and it is impossible to discern in everything going on around us just what will necessarily disappear with the revolution itself, and what will remain in its wake.

The world that is emerging is still half buried in the wreckage of the world that is dying, and in the middle of the immense confusion that human affairs present, no one can say what will remain of the old institutions and the old ways, and what will simply disappear.

Although the revolution taking place in government, laws, ideas, and the attitudes of men is still far from over, it is impossible even now

Chapter 34 appeared as Volume II, Part IV, Chapter 8 in the original, complete text.

to compare the results with anything the world has ever seen before. If I go back over all the centuries since antiquity, I find nothing comparable to what I see around me today. The past sheds no light on the future; the mind gropes in the dark.

Yet even in the midst of this vast scene, so new and confusing, I begin to glimpse the outline of a few principal features.

I see that the benefits and the evils are about equal in the world. Great wealth is disappearing; the number of small fortunes is growing; needs and pleasures multiply; there are few who are extremely wealthy and few who are hopelessly poor. Ambition is almost universal but rarely very far-reaching. Individuals are isolated and weak whereas society is quick, farsighted, and powerful; individuals are engaged in small activities, the State in large ones.

Spirits are not bold, but morals are agreeable and laws humane; if there are few examples of great devotion, or of noble, brilliant, and pure courage, violence is rare, cruelty almost unknown. Human lives are longer and property is secure. Life is plain, but comfortable and very calm. Pleasures are neither very cultured nor very cruel, manners are not refined and tastes not very crude. Few men are very learned nor are populations very ignorant. Genius is rare and enlightenment more common. The human spirit develops in small projects undertaken cooperatively, and not by the strength of will of a few of them. Men produce little that is perfect, but they produce more. All bonds of race, class and inheritance are loosened; the bond of shared humanity is strengthened.

When I look among all these different features for what seems most general and most striking, I begin to see that what is true in men's fortunes also holds in thousands of other cases. Almost all extremes are blunted; whatever stands out is pared down and replaced by something average, less high as well as less low, less brilliant and less dull than what used to be.

I look around and see that everyone looks the same; no one stands out, either too high or too low. The spectacle of universal uniformity saddens and chills me, and I am tempted to regret the society that has disappeared.

When the world was filled with men both great and small, rich and poor, very wise and very ignorant, I could choose to ignore the second and only see the first, and what I saw pleased me; but I understand that my pleasure was born of weakness; because I am not able to take in everything around me, I could separate what I wished to see from everything else. That is not the way of the eternal and almighty Being whose eye sees all things, who sees clearly the whole human race and every individual.

It is natural to believe that what is most pleasing in the eyes of the creator and preserver of men is not the singular prosperity of the few, but the well-being of all: what seems to me decadent is to him progress; what hurts me is pleasing to him. Equality is less elevated, perhaps, but it is more just, and in justice lie greatness and beauty.

I try to look into the mind of God, and to see and judge human affairs as he does.

There is no one living who can say with certainty that the new state of society is superior to the old; but it is already clear that it is different.

There are certain vices and virtues that were inherent in aristocratic societies that are so foreign to the minds of people today that they could not understand them. There are good and bad instincts that were previously unknown and are natural to people of today; ideas that once seemed natural to some, and are rejected now. These are like two distinct races, each with its advantages and disadvantages, virtues and vices.

We must be careful not to judge the newly emerging societies by the standards of those that no longer exist. That would be unfair, for these two entirely different societies are incomparable.

It is no longer reasonable to ask people today to show the distinctive virtues that were characteristic of the social conditions of their ancestors, because that world has fallen and with it, everything that was once good and bad.

These things are not well understood today.

I see many of my contemporaries who are determined to choose from among the institutions, opinions, and ideas born of the old aristocratic foundation of society; they would like to abandon some but retain others, and carry them into the New World.

I believe that they are spending their time and their energy in a sincere yet fruitless exercise.

It is no longer a matter of retaining some of the positive aspects procured in times of inequality, but of securing the new benefits offered by equality. We ought not try to make ourselves like our fathers, but we must attempt to reach our own style of greatness and happiness.

As for myself, reaching finally the conclusion of my work, and discovering from afar, and all at once, the different things I have observed in the course of it, I am filled with both fear and hope. I see great dangers; great risks to be avoided or minimized, and I grow increasingly strong in the belief that, to be honest and prosperous, democratic nations have only to choose to be.

I am aware that many of my contemporaries believe that mortals here on earth are never masters of themselves, and that they are obliged to obey some mysterious law, unknowing and overpowering, and based on events in the past, on race, sun, or climate.

Those are false and weak doctrines, and can never produce anything but weak men and fearful nations: Providence did not make human beings all free or all slave. Rather, it has drawn a circle of fate around each man from which he may not escape; but, within its wide limits, man is powerful and free; and so are nations.

Nations today are incapable of creating conditions of inequality; but it is up to them whether equality leads them to servitude or freedom, to enlightenment or barbarism, to prosperity or privation.

A Tocqueville Chronology
(1805–1859)

1805   Born in Paris on July 29, the third son of Hervé Tocqueville and his wife Louise-Madeline Le Peletier de Rosanbo.

1821   Secondary education at the lycée in Metz, France.

1824–
1826   Studies law in Paris.

1826–
1827   Travels to Switzerland, Rome, Naples, and Sicily. Keeps a lengthy account of his travels with special interest in the conditions and effects of freedom.

1828–
1832   Appointed a junior magistrate in the courts of law at Versailles.

1830   Charles X, the last Bourbon king, falls and the "July monarchy" of Louis-Philippe begins. The House of Orleans is established.

Decides on August 26 to travel and see the United States. Tocqueville and his companion, Gustave de Beaumont, seek a leave of absence to report on prison reform in the United States.

1831   Tocqueville and Beaumont arrive at Newport, Rhode Island, on May 9.

1832   Tocqueville and Beaumont return to France prematurely in March.

1833   Tocqueville and Beaumont publish *Du Système pénitentiaire aux États-Unis*. Tocqueville makes first trip to England.

1835   Tocqueville publishes Volume I of *Democracy in America*. He marries Mary Mottley, an English woman nine years his senior.

1837   Tocqueville narrowly misses being elected to the Chamber of Deputies.

1838   First American edition of *Democracy in America*. Tocqueville elected to the Academy of Moral and Political Science.

1839   Tocqueville elected to the Chamber of Deputies as the representative of Valognes, a small town near his château at Tocqueville in Normandy. He represents this district until he leaves public life in 1852. Writes his "Report on the Abolition of Slavery."

1840   Tocqueville publishes Volume II of *Democracy in America.*

1841   Tocqueville elected to membership in the prestigious Académie Française.

1848   A revolution proclaims the Second Republic.

1849   Tocqueville makes his first trip to Germany.

1849   Tocqueville serves as Minister for Foreign Affairs, June–October.

1850–
1851   Tocqueville writes his *Recollections* of the events of 1848–1850 while in Italy recuperating from a severe attack of tuberculosis.

1851   A coup by President Louis-Napoléon Bonaparte. Tocqueville protests the coup and is briefly imprisoned.

1852   Louis-Napoléon proclaims himself Emperor Napoléon III. The Second Empire is established.

1856   Tocqueville publishes *The Old Regime and the Revolution.*

1859   Tocqueville dies of tuberculosis on April 16 at Cannes, France. He is buried three weeks later at his chateau in Normandy.

Questions for Consideration

1. What does Tocqueville believe are the basic requirements for a successful democracy?

2. How does Tocqueville define democracy, equality, liberty, and tyranny of the majority? Does he tend to use those word concepts fairly consistently, or does his meaning seem to vary from time to time?

3. Is Tocqueville hopeful about the prospects for democracy in the United States because of its political institutions or because of the social conditions, assumptions, and relations that he observed?

4. What does Tocqueville view as the disadvantages or dangers of democracy? For example, why are the best-qualified people not likely to assume positions of leadership in public life?

5. Tocqueville is well remembered because of his concern about the possibility of a "tyranny of the majority." What are his reasons? Do they seem well-founded in the American case? Why shouldn't majority rule be inevitable in a democratic society?

6. Tocqueville introduced the word-concept *individualism* into modern discussions of the self in society. What exactly did he mean by it? What apprehensions did he associate with the possible excesses of individualism?

7. Tocqueville encountered a very religious country divided into many different denominations, continuously swept by evangelical revivals. How does he assess the relationship between religion and democracy in the United States? What relation does he see between religious vitality and the separation of church and state in the United States? Does he find a penchant for tolerance or intolerance?

8. It has been said that the highest good (or greatest goal) in Tocqueville's mind was the achievement of liberty. Do you feel that the achievement of liberty was more important to him than building a sense of social connectedness and responsibility? Was it more important than achieving and preserving equality of condition?

9. Tocqueville argued that Americans placed great emphasis and faith in what they called "self-interest well understood." He believed (hoped?)

that the interest of all might benefit. Do you feel that he may have been naïve about human nature, or too idealistic? If people pursue their private interests, is that somehow likely to serve the common good?

10. Was the "sovereignty of the people" a meaningful reality in Jacksonian America, or is it more of a rhetorical flourish, a concept largely theoretical?

11. Tocqueville believed that the moral authority of the majority was good, but that tyranny by the majority was bad. Are these views in conflict?

12. Tocqueville lamented the lack of "independent minds" in democratic America. Do you agree with this belief, and, if so, is that an inevitable result of an egalitarian society? Could American thought and culture have been so lacking in diversity and conflict as Tocqueville believed?

13. Do you feel that Tocqueville's assertions are time-specific, or do they transcend the particular circumstances of the Jacksonian era? For example, Tocqueville insisted that American government was happily decentralized, almost to the point of being invisible, but also that it would take on larger responsibilities as time passed.

14. Tocqueville has often been praised as an amazing prophet. What do you see in his background, his visit to the United States, or his broad concerns that might explain that gift?

15. A common criticism of Tocqueville is that he seriously overestimated the nation's and democracy's "equality of condition." Do you agree? Does his use of "equality" contain other meanings?

16. Why does Tocqueville support democracy? Why does he fear it?

17. Why is Tocqueville so skeptical about the wisdom of placing excessive power (sovereignty) in the hands of the people?

Selected Bibliography

TOCQUEVILLE'S WRITINGS

Memoir, Letters, and Remains of Alexis de Tocqueville. Edited by Gustave de Beaumont. Cambridge: Macmillan, 1861, 2 vols.

Tocqueville, Alexis de. *Democracy in America and Two Essays on America*. Edited by Isaac Kramnick. New York: Penguin Books, 2003.

Tocqueville, Alexis de. *The Old Regime and the Revolution*. Edited by François Furet and Françoise Melonio. Chicago: University of Chicago Press, 1998.

Tocqueville, Alexis de. *Selected Letters on Politics and Society*. Edited by Roger Boesche. Berkeley: University of California Press, 1985.

Tocqueville, Alexis de. *Writings on Empire and Slavery*. Edited by Jennifer Pitts. Baltimore: Johns Hopkins University Press, 2001.

University of Virginia American Studies hypertext project, *Democracy in America* with supplementary materials, University of Virginia, http://xroads.virginia.edu/~HYPER/hypertex.html.

BIOGRAPHICAL AND CRITICAL WORKS

Allen, Barbara. *Tocqueville, Covenant, and the Democratic Revolution: Harmonizing Earth with Heaven*. Lanham, Md.: Rowman & Littlefield, 2005.

Amos, S. Karin. *Alexis de Tocqueville and the American National Identity: The Reception of "De la Démocratie en Amerique" in the United States in the Nineteenth Century*. Frankfurt: Peter Lang, 1995.

Boesche, Roger. *The Strange Liberalism of Alexis de Tocqueville*. Ithaca, N.Y.: Cornell University Press, 1987.

Brogan, Hugh. *Alexis de Tocqueville: A Life*. New Haven, Conn.: Yale University Press, 2007.

Drescher, Seymour. *Dilemmas of Democracy: Tocqueville and Modernization*. Pittsburgh: University of Pittsburgh Press, 1968.

Drolet, Michael. *Tocqueville, Democracy and Social Reform*. New York: Palgrave Macmillan, 2003.

Eisenstadt, Abraham, ed. *Reconsidering Tocqueville's* Democracy in America. New Brunswick, N.J.: Rutgers University Press, 1988.

Goldstein, Doris S. *Trial of Faith: Religion and Politics in Tocqueville's Thought.* New York: Elsevier, 1975.

Jardin, André. *Tocqueville: A Biography.* New York: Farrar, Straus and Giroux, 1988.

Kammen, Michael. *Alexis de Tocqueville and* Democracy in America. Washington, D.C.: Library of Congress, 1998.

Kann, Mark E. *Punishment, Prisons, and Patriarchy: Liberty and Power in the Early American Republic.* New York: New York University Press, 2005.

Lamberti, Jean-Claude. *Tocqueville and the Two Democracies.* Cambridge, Mass.: Harvard University Press, 1989.

Lawler, Peter Augustine. *The Restless Mind: Alexis de Tocqueville on the Origin and Perpetuation of Human Liberty.* Lanham, Md.: Rowman & Littlefield, 1993.

Lively, Jack. *The Social and Political Thought of Alexis de Tocqueville.* Oxford: Clarendon Press, 1965.

Mancini, Matthew. *Alexis de Tocqueville and American Intellectuals from His Time to Ours.* Lanham, Md.: Rowman & Littlefield, 2006.

Masugi, Ken, ed. *Interpreting Tocqueville's* Democracy in America. Lanham, Md.: Rowman & Littlefield, 1991.

Melonio, Françoise. *Tocqueville and the French.* Charlottesville: University Press of Virginia, 1998.

Mitchell, Harvey. *America after Tocqueville: Democracy against Difference.* New York: Cambridge University Press, 2002.

Nolla, Eduardo, ed. *Liberty, Equality, Democracy.* New York: New York University Press, 1992.

Pierson, George Wilson. *Tocqueville and Beaumont in America.* New York: Oxford University Press, 1938; reprinted by Johns Hopkins University Press as *Tocqueville in America*, 1996.

Reeves, Richard. *American Journey: Traveling with Tocqueville in Search of Democracy in America.* New York: Simon & Schuster, 1982.

Schleifer, James T. *The Making of Tocqueville's* Democracy in America. Chapel Hill: University of North Carolina Press, 1980.

Siedentop, Larry. *Tocqueville.* Oxford: Oxford University Press, 1994.

Tocqueville Review. Charlottesville, Va.: The Tocqueville Society, Fall 1979–, 27 volumes to date.

Welch, Cheryl B. *De Tocqueville.* Oxford: Oxford University Press, 2001.

Wolin, Sheldon S. *Tocqueville between Two Worlds: The Making of a Political and Theoretical Life.* Princeton, N.J.: Princeton University Press, 2001.

Zetterbaum, Marvin. *Tocqueville and the Problem of Democracy.* Stanford, Calif.: Stanford University Press, 1967.

Index

abolitionism, 8
absolute monarchy, 77, 78–79
  material prosperity and, 134, 135
Académie Française, 27
Academy of Moral and Political Science,
  27, 171
Adams, John Quincy, 13
administrative centralization
  defined, 58–59
  in England, 59
  newspapers and, 121–22
administrative decentralization
  defined, 21
  political effects of, 58–62
  townships and, 57–58
  in the U.S., 60–62
administrative instability, 71–73
African Americans
  democracy and, 17–18
  family of, 93
  independence of, 93
  oppression of, 92–93
  revolution and, 155
  slavery and, 92–95
  status of, 91–92, 94, 95
Albany, New York, 11, 30
alcohol control, 119
Alger, Horatio, 25
ambition, 153–54
American character. *See* national character
American flag, 30
American Revolution
  national character and, 46–47
  popular sovereignty and, 54
anarchy
  equality and, 162
  fear of, 136
  intellectual, 157
  tyranny and, 80–81
  voluntary association and, 126
ancient times
  historians in, 108–9
  Roman Empire, 163

Anglo-Americans
  national character and, 45
  religious beliefs, 86
  social conditions, 46–53
  Tocqueville's definition of, 20–21
apprenticeships, 51
arbitrary power, 75–76
architecture, 105
aristocracy
  absence of, 46, 52
  in the American West, 50–51
  arts and, 102, 105
  classes in, 110
  in colonial America, 25
  democracy and, 27–28, 39, 55
  democratic revolution and, 111–12
  diversity and, 153
  in England, 74
  family and, 111
  historians and, 106–9
  individuals in, 106–8, 110
  industrialization and, 137–40
  inheritance laws and, 47–48
  juries and, 83
  landed, 138–39, 140
  laws of succession and, 47–50
  literary production and, 105
  majority and, 71
  manufacturing, 139–40
  marriage and, 146–48
  persuasion in, 157
  status in, 158
  voluntary associations and,
    117–18
  women and, 146
armed forces, 60
artisans, 104
arts
  aristocracy and, 102, 105
  cultivation of, 101–6
  quality of, 102–4
association, freedom of, 122, 124,
  125–26

associations, 116–19. *See also* political
associations; voluntary associations
proliferation of, 21

Baltimore, 14
Beaumont, Gustave de, 171
aristocratic lineage, 5
friendship with de Tocqueville, 5
"Guide and the Osier Bottle, The"
(drawing), 12*f*
plans for U.S. trip, 7–8
portrait of, 6*f*
return to France, 10
slavery and, 8, 10, 14
U.S. travels, 10–14
Beecher, Catharine, 29
beliefs
democracy and, 99–100
in democratic countries, 156
equality and, 99–100
shared, 98
sources of, 98–101
Bellah, Robert, 30
bicameralism, 25
Boston, 13

Cabanis, Pierre, 88
Canada, 13
Catholic community, 13
central (federal) government
strength of, 24
in the U.S., 60–62, 61–62
centralization. *See also* administrative
decentralization; government
centralization
administrative, 58–59, 121–22
defined, 58–59
in Europe, 61
change, in democracies, 156
Channing, William Ellery, 13
Charles X, 3, 171
chastity, 145
Christian religions. *See also* religion
belief in, 86
despotism and, 163
equality and, 38, 40
freedom and, 87
power of, 85
citizen participation, 5
civil associations, 5, 116. *See also* voluntary
associations
ineffectiveness of, 124
civil juries, 83–84
Civil War, 30
cold war, 31
colonial America
democracy in, 25
national character and, 46–47
Commentaries on American Law (Kent), 17
common good, 113, 115, 127
community, sense of, 57

Constitution, France, 25
Constitution, U.S., 25
instability of, 72
state governments and, 56
county government, 56, 57
courtier spirit, 78–80
Creek Nation, 95
crime, 6–7
criminal cases
judges and, 83–84
jury system and, 81–82
criticism, patriotism and, 65
customs, 17

decentralization
administrative, 21, 58–62
government, 21
in the United States, 1
decision making, equality and, 164–65
democracy
abuse of power in, 80–81
advantages of, 63–69
aristocracy and, 27–28, 39, 55
arts and, 102–6
attitudes toward, 96–97
beliefs and, 99–100, 156
change and, 156
characteristics of, 41–42
in colonial America, 25
consensus about, 23
customs and mores and, 17
equality and, 41
family and, 110–11
in France, 18–19, 39
geography and, 17
historians and, 106–9
individuals in, 106–8, 109–12
industrialization and, 137
law and, 17
limitations of, 67–68
literary production and, 105–6
materialism and, 68–69
monotony in, 153
oppression and, 164
persuasion in, 157–58
political process and, 67
productivity and, 68, 137
public opinion in, 158–59
religion and, 16, 84–88, 89–90
social equality and, 17
spread of, 38–39
thinking and, 158
Tocqueville's attitudes toward, 19–20,
27–29
tyranny of the majority in, 16, 74–75
valet mentality in, 79
voluntary associations and, 117–19
Democracy in America (Tocqueville)
balance of, 27–28
content and themes, 15–26
contributions of, 1–2

French audience for, 15
inaccuracies in, 1–2
legacy of, 29–31
predictions in, 29–31
response to, 19–20, 26–29
sources for, 23–24
translations of, 27
Democracy in America, Volume I
    (Tocqueville)
  freedom of the press covered in, 23
  Introduction to, 16, 37–42
  predictions in, 31
  publication of, 171
  response to, 18, 26–29
  themes, 15, 25
Democracy in America, Volume II
    (Tocqueville)
  evaluation of U.S. in, 22
  preface to, 19
  publication of, 172
  response to, 26–27
  themes, 15, 25, 42
  writing of, 26*f*
"democratic envy," 30
democratic institutions
  equality and, 161–62
  in Europe, 90–91
  in France, 15
  individualism and, 112–16
  industrialization and, 67
  religion and, 87
  revolution and, 155
democratic revolution
  African Americans and, 155
  equality and, 155
  growth of, 37–38
  individualism and, 111–12
  inevitability of, 18–19, 96–97
  meaning of, 22
  minorities and, 155
  rarity of, 154–61
  restlessness and, 155
  wealthy people and, 114–15
despotism
  equality and, 113–14, 163–64
  liberty and, 113
  majority and, 77
  materialism and, 136
  religion and, 88
  types of, 162–67
  vulnerability to, 162
diversity
  in aristocracy, 153
  disappearance of, 154
division of labor, 138, 139
  among women and men, 150
doctrinal beliefs, 98
dogmatic beliefs, 98
Durkheim, Émile, 2
Du Système pénitentiaire aux Etats-Unis
    (Tocqueville and Beaumont), 171

Eastern State Penitentiary, 14
economic conditions, equality in, 17
education
  equality and, 51
  jury system and, 82–83
  level of, 22
  political associations and, 124
  of women, 140–42, 143, 147
egoism, 110, 112
elected leadership, 115
England
  administrative centralization in, 59
  aristocracy in, 74
  inheritance laws, 50
  judges in, 83–84
  mixed government in, 74
  voluntary associations in, 117
  women in, 145
enlightened self-interest, 25, 127–28
Enlightenment, 2, 3, 16
entail, 24
equalitarian, 18
equality. *See also* social equality
  anarchy and, 162
  beliefs and, 99–100
  benefits of, 169–70
  decision making and, 164–65
  democracy and, 41, 161–62
  despotism and, 113–14, 163–64
  education and, 51
  effects of, 96
  influence of, 37–38
  inheritance laws and, 48
  intellectual, 51, 157
  liberty and, 21
  majority and, 70
  materialism and, 30
  political consequences of, 52–53
  religion and, 38, 40
  restlessness and, 133
  revolution and, 155
  social conditions and, 46
  voluntary associations and, 117,
    119, 135
  of women and men, 149–52
"equality of condition," 24
Europe
  centralization in, 61
  democratic institutions in, 90–91
  equality of women and men in, 149–50
  family in, 85–86
  freedom of speech in, 76
  morality in, 148–49
  national character, 44
  women in, 141, 143, 145, 149–50, 151
executive power, 1

family
  aristocracy and, 111
  democracy and, 110–11
  in Europe, 85–86

family (*continued*)
  inheritance laws and, 49–50
  marriage and, 146–48
  perpetuation of, 49
  in the U.S., 85–86
federal government
  role of, 57
  strength of, 24
  structure of, 56
fidelity, 22, 146, 147
fine arts, 104–5
Fourth of July celebration, 30
France
  Constitution, 25
  democracy in, 18–19, 39, 155
  democratic institutions in, 15
  freedom in, 88, 115–16
  government centralization in, 59
  individual liberty in, 1
  inheritance laws and, 47–48
  judges in, 83
  national character of, 20
  patriotism in, 30, 63
  political instability in, 1
  popular sovereignty and, 18
  prisons in, 6–7
  religious freedom in, 15
  response to *Democracy in America*
    by, 15
  royal infallibility in, 70
  social equality in, 115–16
  suicide in, 134
  Tocqueville's return to, 10
  women in, 141
freedom
  of association, 122
  in France, 88, 115–16
  majority control and, 76–78
  minimizing the risks of, 125
  of the press, 23
  religion and, 87–88
  of speech, 76–77
  of thought, 23, 76–78
  wealth and, 135
  of women, 140–41, 146–47
  writers and, 77–78
free institutions, 161–62
French Revolution
  Tocqueville family and, 2–3
frontier women, 143

Garrison, William Lloyd, 8
"general ideas," 22
geography, democracy and, 17
girls. *See* women
government
  concentration of authority, 59, 67–68
  voluntary associations and, 118–19
government centralization
  defined, 58–59

  in France, 59
  in the U.S., 59–60
government decentralization, 21
"Guide and the Osier Bottle, The"
  (Beaumont), 12*f*
Guizot, François, 3

Hall, Basil, 27
historians
  in ancient times, 108–9
  in aristocratic centuries, 106–9
  in democratic centuries, 106–9
  individuals and, 106–8
human fellowship, 110
human spirit, 168

ideas, newspapers and, 120–22
immigrants, national character and, 44–45
Indians. *See* Native Americans
individualism
  in aristocracy, 153
  associations and, 21
  defined, 109–10
  democracy and, 109–12
  democratic revolution and, 111–12
  family and, 49
  minimizing with free institutions,
    112–16
  newspapers and, 120
  privatization of, 29–30
  public opinion and, 100
  self-interest and, 126–29
individuals
  desire to be led, 165–66
  influence of, 106–9, 158
  isolation of, 112, 168
  state government and, 114
  voluntary associations and, 117
industrialization
  aristocracy and, 137–40
  democracy and, 137
  democratic institutions and, 67
  enterprises, 125
  liberty and, 134
  worker status and, 138
inheritance laws
  American Revolution and, 54
  in England, 50
  in France, 49–50
  land ownership and, 46–50
  love of money and, 50
  self-interest and, 49
intellectual anarchy, 157
intellectual inequality, 51

Jackson, Andrew, 2, 14, 24
judges, 83–84
jury system
  civil cases and, 83
  criminal cases and, 81–82

defined, 81
judges and, 84
justice and, 73
as a political institution, 81–84
justice
majority and, 73
for minorities, 74–75

Kergorlay, Louis de, 15, 18

labor, division of, 138, 139
La Bruyère, Jean de, 77
La Fayette, M. de, 106
land ownership
in the American West, 50–51
inheritance laws and, 47–50
laws of succession and, 47–52
primogeniture and, 48–49
law, 17
legislation
instability of, 71–72
majority and, 69–71, 75–76
mores and, 82
participation in, 55, 62, 66
Le Havre, 7–8
Le Peletier de Rosanbo,
    Louise-Madeline, 171
liberty
attitudes toward, 30–31
despotism and, 113–14
equality and, 21
in France, 1
industrialization and, 134
material prosperity and, 134–37
morality and, 40
religion and, 16
Tocqueville's definition of, 20
in the United States, 1
literature
production of, 105–6
writers, 78
Livingston, Edward, 14
Lonely Crowd, The (Riesman), 29
Louis-Napoléon Bonaparte, 172
Louis-Philippe, 5, 171
Louis XIV, 59, 77, 80
Louis XVI, 2
Louis XVIII, 3
Luther, Martin, 157

majority
abuse of power by, 73
aristocracy and, 71
change and, 156
ideas out of favor with, 159
juries and, 81–84
legislation and, 69–71, 75–76
legitimacy of, 70
morality and, 70, 76
national character and, 78–80

omnipotence of, 69–81, 100–101
physical power of, 76
power exercised by, 76–78
public opinion and, 71, 76–78
thought control by, 76–78
tyranny of, 16, 22–23, 73–75, 78–80
manufacturing aristocracy, 139–40
map, U.S. travel route, 9*f*
Marie, or Slavery in the United States:
    A Depiction of American Customs
    (Beaumont), 10
marriage
aristocracy and, 146–48
male leadership in, 150–51
purpose of, 146–47
respect for, 85
unhappy, 147
women and, 142–44, 146–47, 150–51
Marryat, Frederick, 27
Martineau, Harriet, 27
Marx, Karl, 2
Maryland, 55
materialism
equality and, 30
government purpose and, 68–69
inheritance laws and, 50
liberty and, 134–37
progress and, 40–41
restlessness and, 131–34
role of, 129–31
melancholia, 134
middle class, 130
Mill, John Stuart, 18, 20
mind control, 23
minorities
armed forces and, 60
equality and, 70
justice for, 74–75
revolution and, 155
Mississippi River, 10
mixed government, 74
moeurs, defined, 17
Molière, 77
monarchy
despotism under, 77
sacrifice of will to, 78–79
money, love of, 22
monotony
in a democracy, 153
restlessness and, 152–54
Montaigne, Michel, 127
Montesquieu, Charles-Louis, 2
morality
in Europe, 148–49
liberty and, 40
of the majority, 23, 70
national character and, 45
political stability and, 16
pursuit of wealth and, 86
religion and, 85–86

morality (*continued*)
  role of, 126
  self-interest and, 128
  slavery and, 40
  social equality and, 145–49
  women and, 140, 145, 148–49
mores, 17, 82
Mottley, Mary, 22, 171

Napoléon, 20
Napoléon III, 20, 172
national character, 20
  of European countries, 44
  immigrants and, 44–45
  juries and, 82
  morality and, 45
  origins of, 43–46
  popular sovereignty and, 45
  religion and, 45
  restlessness, 10, 67
  tyranny of the majority and, 78–80
  of the U.S., 43–46
  valet mentality, 79
"national will," 53
Native Americans
  democracy and, 17–18
  Indian removal policy, 8
  as noble, 94
  oppression of, 93–94
  relocation of, 24
  status of, 91–92, 94
New England townships, 57–58, 60
Newport, Rhode Island, 10
newspapers
  administrative centralization and,
    121–22
  ideas presented through, 120–22
  individualism and, 120
  role of, 21
  voluntary associations and, 120–22
  voting rights and, 121
New York City, 10, 14
New York State, land ownership in, 50
Niagara Falls, 13
Nullification issue, 24

Ohio River, 10
Old Regime and the Revolution, The
  (Tocqueville), 5, 15, 172
oppression
  of African Americans, 92–93
  democracy and, 164
  of Native Americans, 93–94
other-directedness, 29

pace of life
  in Canada, 13
  in the U.S., 10, 13
participation
  in Europe, 90
  in legislation, 55, 62, 66

in public policy, 65–69
  public spirit and, 64–65
Patriot Act, 30
patriotism
  annoying, 65
  criticism and, 65
  expression of, 63–65
  extreme, 30, 63, 65
  in France, 30, 63
  genuineness of, 115
  religion and, 87–88
  Tocqueville's observation of, 11
  true, 80
Philadelphia, 13–14
philosophy, 99
Pierson, George Wilson, 8*n*, 17
political associations, 116. *See also* associa-
    tions; voluntary associations
  as educational, 124
  joining, 123
  voluntary associations and, 122–26
political process
  involvement in, 67
  participation in, 65–69
  social equality and, 52–53
political stability
  in France, 1
  morality and, 16
  in the United States, 1
popular sovereignty, 53–55
  applications of, 55
  concerns about, 22–23
  defined, 15
  future of, 15
  legislation and, 55
  national character and, 45
  origins of, 54
  self-interest and, 54–55
  in U.S. vs. France, 18
  voting rights and, 54
poverty, 130, 131, 138, 168
presidency, 57
press
  freedom of, 23
  role of, 21
primogeniture, 24, 48–49
prisoner discipline, 11
prison reform
  administrative instability and, 72–73
  Tocqueville's study of, 6–7, 10–11, 13–14
Prison Report, 26
privacy, 30
private interest, public interest and,
    25–26, 114
privatization, 29–30
productivity, democracy and, 68, 137
professions, apprenticeships for, 51
progress
  as evil, 40
  materialism and, 40–41
prostitution, 148

public interest, private interest and, 25–26, 114
public officials
  arbitrary power of, 75–76
  motivations of, 113–14
public opinion
  in democracies, 158–59
  faith in, 100–101
  individualism and, 100
  influence of, 100
  power of the majority and, 71, 76–78
  reversals of, 159
  role of, 21, 76
public service, 135
public spirit, 63–65. *See also* patriotism
Putnam, Robert, 30

Quakers, 8
Quebec City, 13

race. *See also* slavery
  affection and, 95
  conditions of, 91–95
  defined, 20–21
  divisiveness of, 30, 92
  Tocqueville's interest in, 8, 14
rape, 151–52
readers, 105
recidivism, 6–7
Recollections (Tocqueville), 172
Reeve, Henry, 19–20
religion. *See also* Christian religions
  belief in, 86
  community cohesion and, 13, 16
  controlling influence of, 86
  democracy and, 16, 89–90
  diversity of, 85
  equality of conditions and, 38
  freedom and, 87–88
  government and, 87
  indirect influence of, 84–88
  marriage and, 143
  morality and, 85–86
  national character and, 45
  patriotism and, 87–88
  power of, 85
  slavery and, 41
  strength of, in the U.S., 88–90
  in the West, 87–88
religious freedom
  in France, 15
  in the U.S., 15–16
"Report on the Abolition of Slavery" (Tocqueville), 172
restlessness, 10, 67
  in a democracy, 158
  equality and, 133
  monotony and, 152–54
  prosperity and, 131–34
  revolution and, 155
  wealth and, 131–34, 153

revolution. *See also* democratic revolution
  rarity of, 154–61
Revolution of 1830 (France), 3
Riesman, David, 29
Robespierre, Maximilien, 3, 20
Roman Empire, 163
Rousseau, Jean Jacques, 2, 3
Russia, 31

Saginaw, Michigan, 13
Second Bank of the United States, 24
Second Empire, 172
seduction, 151
self-interest
  common good and, 127
  doctrine of, 25–26
  enlightened, 127–28
  individualism and, 126–29
  inheritance laws and, 49
  materialism and, 137
  morality, 128
  patriotism and, 115
  popular sovereignty and, 54–55
  role of, 129
  wealth and, 138
self-made men, 25
sexual attraction, 145
Sing-Sing, 10
slavery. *See also* race
  Beaumont's interest in, 8, 10
  effect on African Americans, 92–93, 94, 95
  land ownership and, 47
  morality and, 40
  religion and, 41
  Tocqueville's interest in, 8, 14
sobriety, 119
social classes, 110, 130
social conditions
  democracy and, 46–53
  origins of, 46
  political consequences of, 52–53
social equality. *See also* equality
  democracy and, 17
  effects of, 96
  in France, 115–16
  moral behavior and, 145–49
societal disorders, 85–86
socioeconomic changes, 22
South, 10
Spanish Inquisition, 78
Sparks, Jared, 13, 16, 23, 24–25
speech, freedom of, 76–77
Spencer, John Canfield, 11
Spinoza, Baruch, 88
state governments, 56–62
  citizen interest in, 114
  federal government and, 56
Status Seekers, The (Packard), 30
subjugation, 166
succession, laws of, 47–50
suicide, 134

tax collection, 60
Theory of the Leisure Class (Veblen), 30
thought
    democracy and, 158
    freedom of, 23, 76–78
Tocqueville, Alexis de
    aristocratic lineage, 3
    attention paid to in the U.S., 10
    Beaumont and, 5
    birth of, 3
    criticism of the U.S. by, 27
    death of, 5
    decision to study the U.S., 5–7
    definitions by, 28
    democracy and, 19–20, 27–29
    education, 3
    family, 2–3, 5
    health of, 3, 5
    influence of, 1
    journey to U.S., 7–8
    legal studies, 3, 5
    life and character of, 2–7
    map of U.S. travel route, 8*n*, 9*f*
    nonpartisanship of, 27–28
    notebooks of, 24
    plans for U.S. trip, 7–8
    portrait, 4*f*
    prison reform study, 6–7, 10–11
    religious beliefs, 3, 5, 16
    return to France, 10
    slavery and, 8, 14
    sources of, 23–24
    travels in the U.S., 2, 10–14
Tocqueville, Hervé, 3, 171
Tocqueville, Mary de, 5
Tocqueville Château, 26*f*
townships, 56
    role of, 57–58
    tax collection by, 60
Trollope, Frances, 27
Turner, Nat, slave revolt, 8
tyranny
    anarchy and, 80–81
    arbitrary power and, 75–76
    lack of protections against, 74–75
    materialism and, 136
    public opinion and, 76
    of women, 151
"tyranny of the majority." *See* majority

uniformity, 168
unions, 123
universal suffrage, 18
U.S. Congress, 14
useful arts, 102–4

valet mentality, 79
Veblen, Thorstein, 30
Voltaire, 2, 3
voluntary associations. *See also* civil
        associations
    anarchy and, 126

    aristocracy and, 117–18
    equality and, 117, 119, 135
    government and, 118–19
    illegal, 124
    joining, 123
    newspapers and, 120–22
    political organizations and, 122–26
    role of, 116–19
voting rights
    establishment of, 55
    newspapers and, 121
    popular sovereignty and, 54
    universal suffrage, 18

Washington, D.C., 14
wealth
    disappearance of, 168
    elected leadership and, 115
    freedom and, 133–37
    isolation of wealthy people, 114–15
    liberty and, 134–37
    poverty and, 138
    quest for, 22, 30, 86, 115, 129–31, 132,
        135–37, 153–54
    restlessness and, 131–34, 153
    self-interest and, 138
Weber, Max, 2
Webster, Daniel, 13
West
    land ownership in, 50–51
    religious zeal in, 87–88
white man, race and, 92, 95
wives, 142–44
women
    aristocracy and, 146
    character of, 22
    chastity of, 145
    democracy and, 17–18
    division of labor and, 150
    education of, 140–42, 143, 147
    in England, 145
    equality of, 149–52
    in Europe, 141, 143, 145, 149–50,
        151
    in France, 141
    freedom of, 140–41, 146–47
    frontier, 143
    independence of, 141, 142–44
    marriage and, 142–44, 146–47,
        150–51
    morality and, 140, 145, 148–49
    protection of, 142
    rape of, 151–52
    respect for, 151
    role of, 29
    seduction by, 151
    status of, 152
    tyranny of, 151
    as wives, 142–44
writers
    democracy and, 105–6
    freedom of thought and, 77–78